Bobby Jones and the Quest
for the Grand Slam

CATHERINE M. LEWIS

TRIUMPH
BOOKS
CHICAGO

Library of Congress Cataloging-in-Publication Data

Lewis, Catherine M., 1967–
    Bobby Jones and the quest for the grand slam / Catherine M. Lewis.
      p. cm.
    Includes bibliographical references and index.
    ISBN 1-57243-728-6
     1. Jones, Bobby, 1902–1971. 2. Golfers—Unites States—Biography. I. Title

    GV964.J6L49 2005
    769.352'092—dc22
    [B]

                                2004063759

This book is available in quantity at special discounts for your group or organization. For further information, contact:

Triumph Books
601 South LaSalle Street
Suite 500
Chicago, Illinois 60605
(312) 939-3330
Fax (312) 663-3557

Printed in U.S.A.
ISBN-13: 978-1-57243-728-9
ISBN-10: 1-57243-728-6
Design by Eileen Wagner, Wagner/Donovan Design, Chicago, Illinois

Unless otherwise listed, photographs courtesy of the Atlanta History Center (p. 1), the Jones family (p. iii, p. 77), Special Collections, Robert W. Woodruff, Emory University (p. 3), and the USGA (pp. 2, 26, 27, 50, 51, 76, 114, 115).

Contents

From left: Robert Tyre "Bobby" Jones Jr., Robert Tyre Jones IV, and Robert Tyre Jones III. Photo courtesy of the Jones family.

Foreword

Seventy-five years have passed since my grandfather, Bobby Jones, achieved the impossible—the Grand Slam of golf—by winning the four national championships of Great Britain and the United States in the same year. Since that time major sports records that many considered unassailable have fallen, but the Grand Slam is probably more secure now than in 1930. I would like to take a few paragraphs to briefly outline some reasons why I think this is so and to also highlight some of the things that make Bub's (our family nickname for my grandfather) achievement so remarkable.

Besides the extraordinary skill and endurance that my grandfather demonstrated in winning the Grand Slam, perhaps the most fascinating aspect of his achievement is the fact that he first had the idea to win all four major championships as early as 1926. As soon as he won the "double," both the U.S. Open and the British Open in the same year, two things became apparent to him. First, he knew that he did not want to continue to play tournament golf indefinitely. The pressure of championships was starting to take its toll

on him, and he wanted to get on with the business of developing both his professional career and his family. Second, he began to realize that he could win all four of the championships in the same year. He knew that he had only one, at most two, trips to Europe left in the competitive season, and he decided that the venues for the championships in 1930 offered him the best chance of accomplishing his goal. He kept this plan to himself, not telling even trusted friends such as O. B. Keeler and Grantland Rice.

One other remarkable aspect of Bub achieving the Grand Slam was the pressure placed on him by the timing of the championships. Currently the four tournaments of the professional Grand Slam fall in fairly rapid succession, with The Masters in April, the U.S. Open in mid-June, the British Open in July, and the PGA in early August. The Slam that my grandfather won had a significantly different timetable, one that could only have intensified the psychological pressure that he experienced. In 1930 both British championships occurred almost back to back in May and the U.S. Open was contested in July. Incredibly, the U.S.

Amateur was not held until the end of September, leaving a gap of approximately 10 weeks between the Slam's third and fourth legs. Although Bub kept his plan of winning the Grand Slam to himself, by the time he won the third leg, the U.S. Open at Interlachen, it could no longer be a secret to anyone, including the press, that he stood on the verge of accomplishing something that no one else had ever done. The psychological pressure on him must have been tremendous as the summer gave way to the fall and a Depression-racked country sought stories to capture its imagination and distract it from the precarious times. Fifteen thousand people gathered at the Merion Cricket Club in suburban Philadelphia to watch Bub's final championship. That he was able to withstand the pressure, all the while maintaining his commitment to his law practice and his family, is astounding.

Finally, a word needs to be said about the differences between the Slam of 1930 and the modern Slam. Much has been written about the intensity of the competition in today's Slam, and there is almost an effort to denigrate the quality of the amateur championships. In 1930, however, that was not the case. From the start of championship golf up until the early sixties, amateur championships were in many ways more difficult to win than the Opens for a couple of reasons. First, they required tremendous endurance (as they do to this day). Thirty-six holes of qualifying golf preceded almost seven day's worth of 36-hole matches. It was not uncommon for Bub and other competitors to lose extraordinary amounts of weight in these grueling competitions. Second, the quality of play in the amateur game was in many ways equal to that in the professional game. It was not uncommon in those days for an amateur to win against professionals, something that probably can't happen in major championship golf anymore.

These are just a few of the reasons that I believe Bub's Grand Slam victory will probably stand for all time as one of the great achievements in sports. But more than this, my family and I will always remember the integrity, humor, and intelligence that our grandfather brought to his entire life, and we will remember these as the greatest legacy that he has left to us.

I have known Dr. Catherine Lewis for almost 10 years. We have worked together in the trenches both on the Down the Fairway exhibit and the Bobby Jones Centennial

Dinner at the Atlanta History Center. I have always respected Catherine for her commitment to both her job at the History Center and her scholarship. Her first book on my grandfather, *Considerable Passions*, was thoroughly researched and thoughtfully written. I think the reader will find that this volume is to the same high standard, and I am honored to have been asked to contribute this brief Foreword. It is my hope that it will stand as a meager thanks to Catherine for all that she has done to preserve the legacy of my grandfather, one of the greatest men I have ever known.

—*Dr. Robert Tyre Jones IV*
Atlanta, Georgia

John D. Ames and Jack Nicklaus (right) at the 1959 U.S. Amateur. Nicklaus also won the event in 1961. Photo courtesy of the USGA.

Foreword

When I look back at the infancy of my career in golf, my first hero was Bob Jones. Next to my late father, Charlie Nicklaus, and my longtime instructor and friend Jack Grout, Mr. Jones had the greatest influence on me in the game—and I never saw him hit a single golf shot. But I felt like I lived and relived some of the greatest moments of Jones' career through the eyes and the stories of my father. When just a 12-year-old boy himself, my father first saw Mr. Jones play in the 1926 U.S. Open at Scioto Country Club in our hometown of Columbus, Ohio. Jones won his second Open there, and because Scioto became my home club when I picked up the game at age 10, my father and the members at Scioto used to show me every place Jones hit the ball during that championship victory. My father never lost admiration for his boyhood idol—the man who later became my idol. When Dad and I used to talk about some aspect of golf, Mr. Jones' name inevitably would surface. Jack Grout, who came to Scioto as a teaching professional at the same time I was introduced to the game, often extolled Jones' virtues, so it is no surprise that he loomed large in my imagination. If there was any one player I tried to emulate in my early teens, it was Bob Jones.

Eventually my imagination gave way to reality when I first met Mr. Jones in 1955 at the U.S. Amateur on the James River Course at the Country Club of Virginia in Richmond. He had been invited by the USGA to speak at the players' dinner before the championship on what was the 25th anniversary of his victory at Merion—a win that completed the Grand Slam. At age 15, it was not only the first national championship I qualified for, but I was the youngest player in the field. During a practice round, Mr. Jones had seen me get home in 2 at the 460-yard 18th hole and asked to meet me. Both Dad and I found him approachable, if not engaging, and we talked casually for a while. Finally he turned to me and said, "Young man, there were only a couple of fellas who got home on that hole today, and you were one of them. I'm going to come out and watch you play some more tomorrow."

So here I am, teeing it up in the first round of my first national championship, against Bob Gardner, one of the best amateur players in the country, and all I've ever heard for most of my young life is, "Bobby Jones this . . . Bobby Jones that." Now the great Bob Jones was going to watch me play. Needless to say, my nerves got the better of me. Through 10 holes, I was 1-up in my match before Mr. Jones came riding down the 10th fairway in a golf cart. Over the next half an hour, I proceeded to go bogey, bogey, double-bogey. Mr. Jones turned to my father and said, "I don't believe I'm doing young Jack much good. I think I'd better get out of here." I did eventually regain my composure, but still lost the match, 1-down. When my father told me later why he left, I remember being impressed by Mr. Jones' sensitivity and concern for a mere acquaintance. As our friendship deepened over the years, it was, for me, this kind of thoughtfulness and graciousness to everyone he encountered that continued to shine brightest of his many qualities.

I began my career as an amateur, and throughout 1959 and 1960, the press constantly asked me when I was going to turn professional. To stave them off while I deliberated about what to do, I would often reply, "How, if I turned pro, could I become the next Bob Jones?" That worked for a while, but after my U.S. Amateur victory in 1961, I seriously began to consider making golf my profession. It was a big decision, not nearly as easy at it seems today. My parents, Charlie and Helen Nicklaus, had hoped that I would emulate Mr. Jones, and they sacrificed a lot to make it possible for me to play. As a golfer, I definitely liked being compared to Jones and particularly liked to think that I might someday approach his record. But I also knew that if I wanted to be the best I could in golf, I had to compete against the best—and that meant competing against the professionals. After the 1961 U.S. Amateur, I had a conversation with Mark McCormack about changing my status. Just about then, I received a nice letter from Bob Jones asking me to consider remaining an amateur, but that he would certainly understand if I

chose to turn professional. So in November 1961, I decided to turn professional.

As I look back on my career, the most important championships and victories were the majors. I recognized at an early age that the success of a golfer is usually weighed against his or her performance in the major championships. Thus, the major championships always highlighted my yearly schedule, and throughout my career, I focused much of my preparation around those dates. The majors are the lasting championships. They are the ones people remember, the ones that live on to be told through generations. While every major championship victory remains indelible to me, I have a special place in my heart for The Masters. Coming to Augusta National every year, driving down Magnolia Lane to the clubhouse, seeing the course flanked by all those flowering trees and azaleas, reminds me of the legacy of Mr. Jones and Clifford Roberts. During my earlier trips to The Masters tournament, my father and I used to spend time talking with Mr. Jones in the Jones Cabin, located on the Augusta National grounds, until my dad passed away in 1970. For this and many other reasons, The Masters is my favorite of the four major championships, and I cherish my six wins there.

Many of us in golf, in fact in all sports, owe Bob Jones a great debt. As to his golfing achievements, they were stunning to me as a youngster, and they have remained so, particularly when one considers that he also managed to complete his education, build a family, and begin a career as a lawyer all while competing. My preoccupation with winning the game's four modern major championships was stimulated by Jones' winning of the Grand Slam in 1930. There is no question in my mind that his achievement made me believe that my goal was possible.

In his day, golf's four majors were the U.S. and British Opens, and the U.S. and British Amateurs. During an eight-year period, he won 13 of them, playing mainly as a part-time golfer. In 1973, I broke Jones' record of 13 major championship victories by winning the PGA Championship at Canterbury in my home state of Ohio. It was a bittersweet victory because of the high esteem in which I always held Jones' record. It is hard to believe that 75 years have passed since Bob Jones won the Grand Slam, but time has not diminished the achievement. Nor has the feat been diluted by the fact that the two amateur events that made up Jones' Grand Slam—the U.S. Amateur and British Amateur—have been replaced by

two professional events—The Masters and the PGA Championship—to create the modern-day Grand Slam. I, for one, can say that his four victories in 1930 motivated me, as they probably did many other golfers, both amateur and professional.

For a boy who grew up idolizing the great Bob Jones, and who now has his own children and grandchildren to share the history of this great game with, the chapter that pays tribute to Bob Jones and his remarkable year of 1930 is one that I hope amazes them as much as it has me. This book, *Bobby Jones and the Quest for the Grand Slam,* tells that story, and I hope you enjoy it.

—*Jack Nicklaus*
North Palm Beach, Florida

Acknowledgments

Books are always collaborative ventures, and this one is no exception. I want to begin by thanking the Jones family for their enthusiasm for this project. For this, I am forever grateful. I also would like to recognize the Bobby Jones Executive Committee at the Atlanta History Center, including John P. Imlay Jr. (chairman), Charles R. Yates, Gene McClure, Linton Hopkins, Marty Elgison, and Sidney L. Matthew for their continued guidance and support. Jack Nicklaus, William C. Campbell, and Bob Jones IV deserve special recognition for their contributions to this volume. I would also like to thank Scott Tolley for his continued assistance.

In 2005, this book will be part of a yearlong celebration of the 75th anniversary of the Grand Slam. It will accompany a traveling exhibition developed by the Atlanta History Center that will be on view at the U.S. Open, the British Open, the U.S. Amateur, and the Tour Championship. It will also be seen at the Atlanta History Center's Swan Ball in April and the Atlanta Athletic Club's September Celebration. The book and exhibition play an important role in preserving the Jones legacy, and I am grateful to have had an opportunity to be a part of such a worthy endeavor.

The USGA's contribution to this project is particularly noteworthy. I would like to recognize the Museum and Archives staff, notably Rand Jerris, Nancy Stulack, Patty Moran, and Kim Barney. They worked tirelessly to assist with locating and scanning images, some of which have never been seen, and have been a valuable resource in the world of golf. I would also like to recognize Peter Lewis, the director of the British Golf Museum in St. Andrews, Scotland. He contributed some important stories, and for this I am forever grateful. Over the years, we have had many opportunities to discuss golf history, always with good humor.

I owe a particular debt to numerous individuals who helped to confirm facts or identify photographs. I would like to recognize Teresa M. Burk and Naomi Nelson of the Special Collections Department of the Robert W. Woodruff Library at Emory University; Marjorie Nunn in Institutional Advancement at Emory University; Jarrett Bockler, Bert Hand, and Kathy O'Donnell at Bobby Jones Sportswear and Hartmarx; Ian Ferguson at Georgia Tech; Eddie Papczun at Golf Links to the Past; Walter Rosenthal at Bobby Jones Golf; Kim Dawson of *Bobby Jones—Stroke of Genius*; Barbara Brooks at the Imlay Foundation; and Anne Wade and Annie Cocherty at the Scottish Screen Archive.

I am grateful that Mitch Rogatz, Tom Bast, and Linc Wonham at Triumph Books approached me about doing a book on this important anniversary in the world of sports. I had not planned to do a second Jones book so soon, but they made a very persuasive argument that convinced me that this would be a worthy endeavor. I would mainly like to recognize Jess Paumier and Kelley Thornton for their hard work and dedication in pulling everything together. Anyone who has written a book knows that good editors are a rare breed. I have been fortunate to have found, twice now, fine ones at Triumph. I would also like to thank Eileen Wagner for her elegant design.

I would also like to express my gratitude to Rich Skyzinski, who served as my fact checker for the second time and Andrea Bates at Alston + Bird LLP for her sound and sensible advice. The staff at the Atlanta History Center deserves special attention, notably Andy Ambrose,

Hillary Hardwick, Deborah Thomas, Heather Howell, and especially Barry Watts. There is no finer group of people working in a history museum in America.

My personal debts are always as significant as my professional ones. My family, Betty, Richard, and Tony Lewis and Shelley Andrew, offered continued encouragement. My friends, Jessica and Will Gaines, Debra Dobkins, Lisa Littlefield and David Tulis, Lynn Watson-Powers, Laura and Elliott Bendoly, and so many others kept me sane while I was working on three books that all seemed to have impossible deadlines.

Finally, I owe my greatest debts to my dear husband John Companiotte, who has dedicated much of his personal and professional life to golf. His love, support, and keen editorial eye made this all possible.

Georgia amateur Thomas Barnes Sr. (left) with William C. Campbell at the opening of the Atlanta History Center's Down the Fairway with Bobby Jones exhibit. Photo courtesy of the Atlanta History Center.

Introduction

Writing an introduction for this book commemorating Bob Jones' improbable Grand Slam is a humbling opportunity to pay my respects to that great golf champion and exceptional human being whom I had the pleasure of knowing from 1950 on.

Dr. Catherine Lewis has brought her professional skills, historical perspective, and informed insights to bear on a favorite subject. And Jack Nicklaus' gracious Foreword reflects his deep admiration of the great man. So I am doubly honored and pleased by this assignment. I've long held Bob Jones in high regard and respected his legacy that character does matter and is basic to golf as a game built on honor and appealing to the best in human nature. He showed the world how to play golf both superbly and as a game, and also how to behave as a golfer, playing all out but with courtesy to everyone. As we have seen in Palmer, Nicklaus, Watson, etc., this "amateur spirit" is not limited to amateurs—the vital factor obviously being love of golf as a game.

Golf's growth peaked in 1997—Tiger Woods' first year as a professional, when he took The Masters by storm. But many of the newcomers have drifted away, offsetting yearly gains, so that golf's net numbers have languished. It seems that many newcomer-departees had not realized the game's difficulty or cost in time and money and did not feel welcome or know golf's rules, history, customs, or heroes. So I consider this book about Bob Jones and his legacy both relevant and timely.

Two episodes in recent years have disturbed me in this respect. One was the aftermath of my talk about Bob Jones to a large junior tournament dinner, when a past champion thanked me for telling about Mr. Jones, the designer of a favorite course—obviously meaning Robert Trent Jones—amazingly not knowing the difference between the two men despite always living in Georgia and being a graduate of Georgia Tech!

The other episode was my attendance at a movie theater last spring to see *Bobby Jones—Stroke of Genius*, which I enjoyed, but I was virtually alone in the theater. When it developed that pitifully few people nationally saw that movie, my sad conclusion was that not many people—and indeed few young ones—now even know of Bob Jones, let alone what he accomplished in golf 75 years ago and what he stood for as a person.

I have had to interpret both episodes as evidence of a generational disconnect, calling for more and better awareness of Bob Jones and his legacy. So this book is fortuitous, and I hope that it will be widely read so that neither Bob Jones nor his Grand Slam will be unknown to the very people to whom the story of his golf and his life could mean so much.

I am undiminished in my high opinion of his incomparable competitive record and the personal qualities that enhance his hero status—a Caledonian icon, no less, combining the qualities of modesty, charm, humor, integrity, intellect, grace, and sensitivity in an educated and cultured Renaissance man, but also with a volatile nature that he learned to control and sublimate to the demand and standards of world-class competition. He emerged from the process as a paragon of golf's essential civility and the game's true spirit as embodied in its ancient and honorable traditions. By age 28, he had reached the mountaintop, so he simply resigned from competition. His supreme skills doubtless could have prevailed longer, but he knew that as a person he would not thrive in the constant pressure and concentric life of a full-time career golfer. Besides, he had other interests to pursue.

In recognition of his rare qualities of mind, heart, and character, and particularly his unfailing consideration of others, 50 years ago the United States Golf Association established, as its highest individual honor, the Bob Jones Award, presented yearly "for distinguished sportsmanship." And readers of the *Atlanta Constitution* voted Bob Jones as the South's outstanding person of the first half of the 20th century—not the best golfer, which was a given, but the best person. Thanks to the his fame (with a tip of the cap to O. B. Keeler), he was widely celebrated as a great champion and truly appreciated for the high moral values that he lived by. He was, in all respects, an innate gentleman. I like to think that his legacy as golf's greatest role model will live on, long after we are gone.

I am a relic of a time when amateur golf was a goal in itself, to be pursued and savored all of one's life, rather than used as a step to something else; I still believe it. But amateur golf has changed, primarily because of the fame and fortune possible on the PGA Tour commanding so much public attention. My sense, however, is that amateur golf—and the "amateur spirit"—can also thrive even without media glare because the amateur game really belongs to the changing cast of players who still flock to amateur events and still strive for Walker Cup team selection. I think Bob Jones would approve.

—William C. Campbell
Huntington, West Virginia

Bobby Jones and the Quest
for the Grand Slam

~*1*~

A Hero Mightily
Esteemed

> *"It would be only natural to assume that Jones was purely and simply a genius at golf, that he was a man who could step onto a course at any given occasion and handle a club as though it were an obedient extension of his imagination."*
>
> —CHARLES PRICE

LEGENDARY SPORTS HEROES, names long recorded in the annals of American history—Babe Ruth, Johnny Weissmuller, Bill Tilden, Charles Paddock, Gertrude Ederle, and Red Grange—dominated the twenties. Writing for the *Atlanta Constitution* in 1958, Drew Middleton described Robert Tyre "Bobby" Jones Jr.'s membership in that illustrious group: "Jones was an integral part of the first great birth of American sports enthusiasm, the golden decade of the twenties. Those who cannot remember the fluent precision of Jones' putting, or Babe Ruth standing at the plate, or Jack Dempsey leaping snarling from his corner are the poorer." Although dozens of male and female athletes excelled in that decade, none captured the public imagination quite like Jones. Though it took him seven years to win his first major title, he played in 31 championships and placed first or second better than 50 percent of the time. Jones won five of the eight U.S. Amateurs he entered after 1922. He won one of the three British Amateurs in which he competed. In the U.S. Open, between 1922 and 1930, he finished first or second every year except 1927. He won three of the four British Opens he entered. He became the first golfer to win both open championships in a single year. He became, and remains, the only golfer to win the Grand Slam, taking the British Amateur, the British Open, the U.S. Open, and the U.S. Amateur in a single year. In *Triumphant Journey*, Richard Miller concluded, "In the Golden Age of Sport, his name shone the brightest."

Jones was a consummate amateur, believing that sport should build character and not be played for money. Jones makes his position clear in *Golf Is My Game*:

Throughout all the period when I was competing in golf tournaments, I played as an amateur. My father was not a rich man, and I have no doubt that the expense of even the little traveling I did to golf tournaments sometimes became troublesome. But there had never been any thought in the mind of either of us that I should ever play golf as a professional. Even the accomplishment of the Grand Slam made no change in our attitudes upon this point.

But amateurism was not just about money. Drawing on the British tradition, amateur athletes were cautious not to seize advantages that were unavailable to their fellow competitors and shied away from gamesmanship. In golf, both amateurs and professionals relied upon an individual's adherence to the rules. But amateur players subscribed to a slightly different philosophy than professionals. In *Ethics in Sport*, Nicholas Dixon argues that unlike cheating, gamesmanship includes "using legal but morally dubious tactics designed to unsettle opponents."

In *Golf and the American Country Club*, historian Richard J. Moss also identifies country clubs as important sites where the amateur ideal was perpetuated. Growing out of voluntary associations that had their roots in the antebellum period, "the country club was an attempt to preserve certain aspects of Victorian culture before they were overrun by new values spawned in the burgeoning

"Golf may be . . . a sophisticated game. At least it is usually played with the outward appearance of great dignity. It is nevertheless a game of considerable passion, either of the explosive type or that which burns inwardly and sears the soul."

—BOBBY JONES

More than any other competitor that Jones faced during his career, Walter Hagen used gamesmanship to his advantage. He was a brilliant match-play competitor who could shatter his opponent's confidence with a flippant remark. Hagen was known to arrive at a tournament, walk to the first tee, and ask loudly enough for all his fellow competitors to hear: "I wonder who's going to take second?" Jones' class status and moral code, modeled on Victorian standards of conduct, made him far too modest to make such a boast. In the United States, amateur associations—the National Association of Amateur Athletes of America (1879), the Amateur Athletic Union (1888), and the United States Golf Association (USGA) (1894)—helped protect and promote this ideal.

industrial city." Early members of such clubs were largely Protestant, affluent leaders of the community, whose social status was solidly established. The growing popularity of golf was the impetus for the founding of numerous country clubs late in the 19th century. Unlike early horse-oriented clubs that required immense amounts of land for fox hunting, golf clubs were comparatively inexpensive to build and maintain. Additionally, golf, like tennis and croquet, was deemed an appropriate sport for both men and women.

Although a handful of private clubs, notably the South Carolina Golf Club and the Savannah Golf Club, introduced golf to America in the late 18th century, golf did not become popular for another century. Sports such as horse

The mule house at the Atlanta Athletic Club's East Lake Golf Course. Photo courtesy of the USGA.

racing and prize fighting held much greater appeal for the masses. Robert Hunter, a socialist reformer, reflected in 1926 on how much the game had changed: "Less than 30 years ago the game was looked upon as something effeminate—an unmanly sport suited to the pink-coated fops and dandies who played it. And what moral courage was required in those days to walk the town streets or board a train dressed in knickers and carrying a bag of clubs." Between 1854 and 1900, more than 125 golf clubs were established in the United States—including Bobby Jones' home club, the Atlanta Athletic Club, in 1898. In 1920, the USGA counted 477 member clubs; by the time Jones won the Grand Slam in 1930, there were more than 1,100 member clubs in the USGA. The United States had more than 5,700 golf courses. The game was quickly embraced by both sexes, who subscribed to the new

Bobby Jones at the age of nine. Photo courtesy of the USGA.

philosophy of physical education, and golfers became, as Scottish-born industrialist Andrew Carnegie once described, "worshipers of God of the open air."

Robert Tyre Jones Jr. was born on March 17, 1902, in a home in Atlanta's Grant Park neighborhood, now the home of the Atlanta Preservation Center, just as golf was growing in stature. As an infant, Jones suffered from such severe stomach problems that until the age of five, he could eat little more than egg whites, pabulum, and black-eyed peas. He was known as Robert to his mother, Rob to his father, Bob to his friends, and Bobby to the public. In the summer of 1907, the Jones family rented several rooms in Mrs. Frank Meador's boarding house, which overlooked the Atlanta Athletic Club's new East Lake Golf Course. Fulton Colville, one of the boarders, cut down a *cleek* (a club with a long, shallow blade that compares to today's 3 iron), giving Jones his first golf club.

As a young boy, Jones followed club professional Stewart Maiden around the course, mimicking his swing. In his 1927 autobiography, *Down the Fairway*, Jones wrote that the arrival of Maiden in 1908 at the Atlanta Athletic Club was "the very luckiest thing that has ever happened to me in golf, which is saying a lot, because my entire career, if it may be called a career, has been lucky." Jones explained, "When I followed Stewart, I didn't carry even one club. I just watched him. I never was conscious of studying his play, or of trying to play like him." In 1911, at the age of nine, Jones won the Atlanta Athletic Club's Junior Championship, defeating Howard Thorne, who was eight years his senior, 5 and 4, during match play. At the age of 11, Jones shot an 80 at East Lake, a course that measured 6,500 yards and had a par of 75. That same year, 1913, Jones watched an exhibition match featuring noted British players Ted Ray and Harry Vardon against local professionals. Jones later remembered being deeply influenced by the way Vardon seemed to ignore his opponent and play against par. Two years later, in 1915, the young Atlantan won his first championship at Druid Hills Golf Club against Archer Davidson, breaking the course record with a 73. By then, Jones had developed a swing that Bernard Darwin would later describe as having "a touch of poetry."

In 1916, at age 14, Jones, who was regularly driving the ball 250 yards, captured the Georgia State Amateur Championship at the Capital City Club's Brookhaven course by beating his friend Perry Adair, who was 16. Impressed by the two boys' caliber of play, USGA committeeman Ralph Reed encouraged them to compete in the U.S. Amateur, which required a handicap of 6 or under and a $5 registration fee. George Adair, Perry's father, assured Jones' father that he would chaperone the two boys, to which the elder Jones consented. Jones, traveling outside the South for the first time, was thrilled. He knew that only one player in five actually qualified, and he later joked that he "hadn't the sense or experience enough to

Jones, the youngest player in the event, faced Eben Byers, the 1906 U.S. Amateur champion and one of the oldest players in the field. Both players had trouble controlling their tempers and were prone to throwing their clubs. Jones finally won the match, 3 and 2. He would joke many years later that the only reason he won was because Byers had run out of clubs. In the next match, Jones beat Frank Dyer, the Pennsylvania state champion, 4 and 2, to get into the quarterfinals. Ultimately, Jones lost to reigning U.S. Amateur champion and a former track star from Yale University, Robert A. Gardner, 5 and 3. Years later, Jones reflected on that finish: "Of all the luck I've had, and I've had a lot, the best luck is that I didn't win at Merion as a kid of 14 at my first Amateur. . . . I might have got the idea that it was an easy thing to do." At the ripe old age of 14, Jones had won the Georgia

"He combined exquisite artistry with utterly relentless precision in a way not quite given to other golfers. Just to see him swing a club was a joy, and the finest tribute any golfer can receive still is to have some old-timer say, 'He looked like Jones on that one.'"

—*BERNARD DARWIN*

be afraid." Dubbed "the new kid from Dixie" and dressed in long pants and a red-and-white-striped bow tie, Jones led all qualifiers on Merion Cricket Club's West Course with a 74 in the morning round. His afternoon was not as stellar: he carded an 89. But the 163 was good enough to make the cut. Perry Adair was also in the field.

State Amateur and the Southern Amateur and had been a quarterfinalist in the U.S. Amateur. From 1916 to 1922, Jones played in numerous championships, but did not capture a title.

During World War I, the USGA, the Royal & Ancient Golf Club of St. Andrews, and the PGA of America

Bobby Jones, Alexa Stirling, and Perry Adair (below) barnstormed across the country to raise money for World War I relief efforts.
Photo courtesy of East Lake Golf Club.

cancelled the major championships. To raise money for the war effort, those organizations and various private clubs sponsored a series of exhibition matches. In the summer of 1917, Jones and Perry Adair traveled to New York to play in the War Relief International Matches. The two boys lived briefly with Grantland Rice, the sportswriter who had befriended Jones' father when Rice wrote for the *Atlanta Journal* from 1902 to 1906. Sponsored by the PGA of America, the exhibitions pitted the best amateurs in the country, including Charles "Chick" Evans Jr., Francis Ouimet, and Jerry Travers, against the nation's top professionals. In 1918, the sporting goods company Wright and Ditson scheduled Red Cross matches throughout the summer that included Atlantans Jones, Adair, and Alexa Stirling, and Chicago golfer and former Western Women's Open champion, Elaine Rosenthal. The young players, donning red Swiss Guard berets, barnstormed around the nation playing mixed four-ball matches. Despite Jones' successes in these exhibitions, which helped raise nearly $150,000, he was widely criticized by the press for frequently losing his temper when he did not play well.

In 1916, at the Georgia State Amateur Championship, Jones would meet a man that would forever change his life. Born on June 4, 1882, Oscar Bane "O. B." Keeler was the son of a Chicago businessman who moved to Georgia when Keeler was only four years old. The Keeler family eventually settled in Marietta, outside Atlanta, where O. B. graduated from high school. After a decade of drifting between jobs in banking, the railroads, and insurance, Keeler became a staff writer for the *Atlanta Georgian* newspaper on January 4, 1909. In 1910, he moved to the *Kansas City Star*. After three years, Keeler returned to

Bobby Jones (left) and Stewart Maiden, the golf professional at East Lake. Photo courtesy of Special Collections, Robert W. Woodruff Library, Emory University.

His Most Perfect Round
by Arthur Daley

Of all the rounds that Bobby shot over the years, though, the one that has always held me in a grip of utter fascination was one he fashioned at Sunningdale during the British Open Championship of 1926. This was an era, mind you, when par figures were considered reasonably sacred, especially in Britain. Furthermore, play was with wooden-shafted clubs and the wedge had not been invented. So Bobby had none of today's stroke savers. At Sunningdale on that extraordinary day, the Emperor Jones came about as close to perfection as ever can be achieved on a golf course. Par was 72. He left the gallery stunned with a 66. But the details are what put such a strain on credulity. On the outgoing nine Bobby scored a 33. He therefore also had a 33 on the trip in. He had exactly 33 putts and 33 other strokes. He did not have a 2 or a 5 on his card. He had six 4s and three 3s on each nine.

the *Georgian* after working briefly as a Hollywood publicist. During that time, Keeler periodically wrote for Grantland Rice, the editor of *The American Golfer* magazine. In 1920, Keeler joined the staff of the *Atlanta Journal*, where one of his responsibilities was to cover Bobby Jones' tournament

Oscar Bane Keeler devoted much of his career to covering Bobby Jones. Photo courtesy of the Marietta-Cobb Museum of History.

play, an assignment that he later joked lasted 10 years. Keeler was present for each of the 31 championships in which Jones participated, and together they traveled more than one hundred twenty thousand miles. Historian Stephen Lowe explained: "[T]he Keeler relationship was vital to Jones' competitive success." Keeler helped Jones in two important ways. Keeler, functioning essentially as a press agent, meticulously documented and interpreted the golfer's exploits, carefully crafting a public persona for him. Secondly, he served as a sounding board for Jones' emotions and anxiety during competition. Jones later said of the relationship, "Keeler attributed so many fine qualities to me when we were traveling together that ultimately I began to take on some from just the suggestion."

As a young golfer, Jones was a skillful and aggressive player, but still had difficulty controlling his temper.

Calamity Jane

Bobby Jones' famous putter, Calamity Jane, came to America in 1903 from Carnoustie, Scotland, in James Maiden's golf bag. Robert Condie, a master clubmaker from St. Andrews, made the club around the turn of the 20th century. In 1907, Maiden became the head professional at the Atlanta Athletic Club's East Lake course. When Maiden left the club to become the professional at Nassau Country Club in New York, his younger brother, Stewart, took over his responsibilities at East Lake. Stewart befriended Jones and his family, though Jones also remained in touch with James, visiting him often when he was in New York.

The blade of the club had several stamps: One was, "Wm. W. Winton, Acton," referring to the professional for whom the club was made. The second was, "Warranted—Hand Forged" below the rose that was Condie's stamp. "Special" was stamped on the toe, and the words "Calamity Jane" were added later by James Maiden.

Though there is some debate about when Jones actually acquired the putter, the evidence points to a day when he played nine holes with the elder Maiden at Nassau just prior to the 1923 U.S. Open. After watching Jones struggle with his putting, Maiden pulled Calamity Jane out of a barrel in the back of his shop, and Jones promptly sank a long putt. He used the putter to win three major championships: the 1923 U.S. Open at Inwood, the 1924 U.S. Amateur at Merion, and the 1925 U.S. Amateur at Oakmont.

When the face of the putter had worn smooth, Jones consulted J. Victor East, the club designer with Spalding in 1926, who made six duplicates of the club, though the location of all but one remains a mystery. The six new clubs were stamped "Robert T. Jones Jr.," and the same stamp appears on the shaft of the club, near the bottom of the leather grip. Jones used one of the duplicate copies, Calamity Jane II, to win his other 10 major championships, including all four legs of the Grand Slam. In 1931, Spalding began manufacturing replicas of the putter for public sale. The original Calamity Jane was given to Augusta National Golf Club in 1948 and is on display there. Calamity Jane II, presented to the USGA in May 1938, is at Golf House in Far Hills, New Jersey.

Journalists of the period predicted that Jones' lack of maturity would overshadow his tremendous skill. Rice wisely observed, "That one fault could prove to be his greatest hazard." Early in his career, Jones recognized that his tantrums were becoming a source of embarrassment. In the 1921 British Open at St. Andrews they came

The Most Important Shot Bob Jones Ever Played

by O. B. Keeler

Bobby Jones (left) and Al Espinosa at the 1929 U.S. Open. Photo courtesy of Special Collections, Robert W. Woodruff Library, Emory University.

My nomination is a 12-foot putt on the home green at Winged Foot, Mamaroneck, New York, in 1929—not in the Grand Slam year. I'll always regard that putt as what you might call the prelude to the Grand Slam. It was the final round of the U.S. Open. Bob had it in the bag, with a half a dozen holes to play—and then had kicked away six strokes, and now he had that 12-foot putt to tie Al Espinosa. On a green as fast as ice, with a 15-inch "borrow" from the left. . . . I couldn't watch that putt. Al Watrous, Bob's fellow competitor, described it later: "The most perfectly gauged putt I ever saw. If that hole had been a 4¼-inch circle on the green, the ball would have stopped in the middle of it." Well, Bob won the playoff the next day. And the Grand Slam the next year. But if he had missed that 12-footer, I don't believe there would have been any Grand Slam, and the impregnable quadrilateral of golf still would have been vacant.

to a head. Jones opened with a 78 and 74. He finished the first nine holes of the third round with a 46. He began the back nine with a 6 on the par-4 10th hole. On the 11th hole, a par-3, his tee shot landed in a bunker. After three attempts to blast it out, his fourth attempt finally reached the green. Instead of putting out, he pocketed his ball, disqualifying himself from the tournament. He did complete the third round and shot a 72 in the fourth. But his behavior was inexcusable. He later wrote, "I have some sterling regrets in golf. This is the principle regret—that ever I quit in competition. I've often wished I could offer a general apology for picking up my ball. It means nothing to the world of golf. But it means something to me."

After watching Jones play in the 1921 U.S. Open at Columbia Country Club in Chevy Chase, Maryland, Jim Barnes, a noted professional golfer from Cornwall, England, and the eventual victor, reflected on Jones' temper: "Never mind that club throwing and the beatings he's taking. Defeat will make him great. He's not satisfied now with a pretty good shot. He has to be perfect. That's the way a good artist must feel." Jones tied for fifth in that event, with Emmett French and Alex Smith. Smith had been the first golf professional at the Atlanta Athletic Club's East Lake course.

At the U.S. Amateur later that year at St. Louis Country Club, Jones further disgraced himself. In the third round match, against Willie Hunter, he threw his golf club toward his bag after making a poor approach shot, and the club bounced, hitting a woman on the leg. Several weeks later, USGA president George Herbert Walker warned Jones in a letter: "You will never play in a USGA event again unless you can learn to control your temper." Jones ultimately

Bobby Jones and Bobby Cruickshank at the awards ceremony for the 1923 U.S. Open at Inwood. Photo courtesy of Special Collections, Robert W. Woodruff Library, Emory University.

managed to quell his public outbursts through the sheer force of will, but confessed in 1930, "I've never gotten rid of my temper. I still get mad as blazes, but I don't show it; I suppress it." Rice later reflected on Jones' transformation, "He had won his fight. From that point on, one might watch him after playing a bad hole or after a poor stroke and see a smooth, even, unhurried swing that carried no hint of the trouble that had gone before. . . . It was his persistent and finally successful battle for mastery of self that made the vast difference."

While studying English literature at Harvard University, Jones beat Bobby Cruickshank in a playoff at the 1923 U.S. Open at Inwood Country Club to capture his first national title. Jones, who roomed with Francis Ouimet during the event, qualified with a 77 and 79, in the middle of the field. Jones played well. Heading into the final round, he had a 3-shot lead. Though he calculated that he needed a 75 to win, he played badly on the back nine. He took a bogey on the 16th and 17th holes, leaving a difficult finish on 18. A good drive was followed by a second shot that landed 20 yards left of the green. He pitched into a bunker, chip-ped out, and 2-putted for a double-bogey 6. Exasperated by his performance on the last holes, he told Keeler, "I didn't finish like a champion. I finished like a yellow dog." Jones then went to his room at the club to wait to see if Cruickshank could catch him. Cruickshank parred the 17th and birdied the 18th, setting the stage for a playoff the next day.

At 2:00 in the afternoon on July 15, Cruickshank, who was given 10-to-7 odds to win, and Jones began the march to the finish. After the 12th hole, Jones had a 2-stroke lead. That would dissipate with bogeys at 14 and 15. Coming to the final hole, the golfers were tied. Cruickshank drove first, and the ball landed on a road, behind a tree. Jones put his in the right rough. His second shot, a 1 iron, landed within six feet of the pin. Jones had captured his first national championship, thus ending the seven lean years. He had become the fourth amateur in the last nine U.S. Opens to win, after Ouimet in 1913, Travers in 1915, and Evans in 1916. At the trophy ceremony, Keeler reported in *The American Golfer* that Cruickshank graciously praised Jones, "My what a golfer that boy is. He's the greatest champion of them all. To be defeated by him is glory enough." When Jones' father,

Photo courtesy of the Atlanta Athletic Club.

waiting in the offices of the *Atlanta Journal*, heard the news, he boldly shouted: "It has been the ambition of my life to bring a champion to Atlanta. And now, thank God, I've done it!"

Over the next several years Jones became a more mature competitor and began building a championship record. At the 1925 U.S. Open at Worcester Country Club in Massachusetts, Jones displayed an act of sportsmanship

"There were times when I felt that I know less about what I'm doing on a golf course than anyone else in the world."

—*BOBBY JONES*

Jones being carried by enthusiastic fans at Atlanta's Brookwood Station after he won the U.S. Open in 1923. Photo courtesy of Special Collections, Robert W. Woodruff Library, Emory University.

Fellow Atlanta Athletic Club member Watts Gunn (left) and Bobby Jones at the 1925 U.S. Open. Photo courtesy of East Lake Golf Club.

that was widely hailed by his contemporaries. On the 11th hole in the first round, Jones' iron shot put his ball in the tall grass. When he went to address it, the ball moved slightly, prompting Jones to call a penalty stroke on himself. Even as the USGA officials urged him to reconsider because no one had seen what happened, Jones refused to relent. Gene Sarazen, who was competing, later said that it was the "greatest display of sportsmanship I've ever witnessed." The penalty stroke in regulation prevented him from an outright win in 72 holes, and ultimately he lost by 1 stroke in the playoff.

In the final round, eight players were in contention, and it was an impressive list: Hagen, Leo Diegel, Johnny Farrell, Jones, Ouimet, Willie Macfarlane, Sarazen, and Mike Brady. At the end of regulation play, Jones and Macfarlane were tied, prompting a playoff. On Sunday, June 5, they began their battle. By the 14th hole, Macfarlane had the lead. At the end of 18, they were tied with 75s. In the afternoon, Jones surged back to take a 4-shot lead. The players tied on the 17th hole, and on the 18th Macfarlane finished with a 4 to Jones' 5. Macfarlane was awarded $500. Keeler later wrote of Jones' display of sportsmanship on that first day of competition, "There are things in golf finer than winning championships." The decision prevented him from becoming the only golfer to win five U.S. Opens. In 1926, Jones would call a second penalty shot on himself on the 15th hole in the first round of the U.S. Open at Scioto Country Club. Even with the penalty, that time he was the victor.

Jones' sportsmanship was so widely acknowledged that the year he won the Grand Slam he was given the Sullivan Award for his promotion of amateur sports by

From left: Ted Ray, Bobby Jones, James Braid, and Harry Vardon at the British Open in 1926. Photo courtesy of Special Collections, Robert W. Woodruff Library, Emory University.

Bobby Jones receiving the 1927 U.S. Amateur trophy from USGA President W. C. Fownes. Photo courtesy of Special Collections, Robert W. Woodruff Library, Emory University.

the Amateur Athletic Union. Twenty-five years later, the USGA initiated the Bob Jones Award, honoring a person who, by a single act or over the years, emulated Jones' sportsmanship, respect for the game and its rules, generosity of spirit, sense of fair play, and perhaps even sacrifice. Ouimet was the first recipient. In 1966, Jones said, "[T]he quality of sportsmanship is the quality I would most want to be praised for."

From 1923 to 1930, Jones won 13 championships. In *A Golf Story*, Charles Price explained, "From 1923 on, then, it was Jones against anybody; Jones against everybody; Jones, in fact, against the field." His record is even more extraordinary when one considers that Jones never took formal lessons, did not enjoy practicing, and played fewer rounds each year than his contemporaries did.

In 1926, Jones became the first American golfer to win "the double"—both the British Open and U.S. Open. After his retirement, Jones remembered the qualifying round at Sunningdale Golf Club in England as the best of his career. He shot a 66, 6 under par. After winning the British Open at Royal Lytham and St. Anne's Golf Club with a score of 291, Jones was rewarded with his first of two ticker-tape parades in New York City. Mayor Jimmy Walker and Major John Cohen, the publisher of the *Atlanta Journal*, escorted him as confetti rained down and a band played "Glory, Glory to Old Georgia" and "Dixie." *The New York Times* reported that the parade was the "greatest reception in the history of sports."

In July, Jones went on to win the U.S. Open at Scioto with a 293, 1 stroke better than Joe Turnesa. Historian Stephen Lowe explained the strain that this hectic schedule had on Jones: "Within 15 days Jones had won

Jones putting during the 1928 U.S. Open championship at Olympia Fields Country Club. Photo courtesy of the USGA.

Jones defeated T. Philip Perkins, 10 and 9, in the 1928 U.S. Amateur finals at Brae Burn Country Club. Photo courtesy of the USGA.

the British Open, sailed home, endured a ticker-tape parade, and won the U.S. Open." It would be another six years before another player—Sarazen—would match Jones' feat.

In 1927, Jones returned to the Old Course at St. Andrews. The last time he played the Scottish course he withdrew from competition in despair; this time he walked onto the course a mature competitor with two university degrees, a wife, and a young daughter. Jones opened with a 68, and with a 72, 73, and 72 over the next three rounds, he broke the Open record by 5 shots. He was 6 strokes better than Aubrey Boomer and Fred Robson. On the final hole, more than twelve thousand Scots surrounded Jones, prompting Keeler to shout, "My God, they're going to kill him." Instead, Jones and his putter, which he called Calamity Jane, were lofted above the crowd and carried to the clubhouse.

In 1928, Jones played in several exhibition matches and on the victorious Walker Cup team, but mainly he focused his energy on the U.S. Open and U.S. Amateur. In June, he lost the Open at Olympia Fields Country Club near Chicago by a single stroke to Farrell in a 36-hole playoff. In September, at Brae Burn Country Club, Jones defeated T. Philip Perkins, 10 and 9, in the final match. Jones played in only two major championships in 1929, the U.S. Open at Winged Foot Golf Club and the U.S. Amateur at Del Monte Golf and Country Club (known today as Pebble Beach). In New York, he won in the 36-hole playoff against Al Espinosa. In the morning round, Jones shot a 72, then shot a 69 in the afternoon to beat Espinosa by 23 strokes in total. In California early in September at the U.S. Amateur, Johnny Goodman

defeated Jones in the first round. Though unexpected, the loss did not derail Jones' plans to try to win all four majors the next year, a feat he ultimately would achieve. Then, to the surprise of his fans, he retired on November 17, 1930, barely two months after winning the U.S. Amateur at Merion Cricket Club.

Jones' retirement after completing the Grand Slam did not diminish his interest in or contribution to golf. He wrote dozens of newspaper articles and became a regular contributor to Rice's *The American Golfer*. Jones also recorded a national instructional radio program from Atlanta that began on January 15, 1931. The series played for 26

"Tournament golf is to ordinary golf what walking a tightrope is to walking along the ground."

—CHARLES PRICE

Wednesdays and ran for 15 minutes, but they have not been released to the public since they originally aired. During his lifetime, he published four books that are still widely read. In 1927, while Jones was still an active competitor, Minton, Balch and Company published his auto-biography, *Down the Fairway*, written with Keeler with a Foreword by Rice. The book was serialized in *Liberty* magazine and was into its third printing within two months. That summer, he wrote two columns per week for the Bell Syndicate, which he continued until 1935. In 1957, he signed a contract with Doubleday to write *Golf Is My Game*, which sold more than

O. B. Keeler took this photograph of (from left) Harold Lloyd, Will Rogers, Bobby Jones, Douglas Fairbanks Sr., and Fred Stone while Jones was filming a series of instructional short films for Warner Brothers. Photo courtesy of the USGA.

Jones' swing was often used as a model. Photo courtesy of the USGA.

thirty-five thousand copies upon its publication in 1960. In 1964, Jones hired Charles Price, the noted editor of *Golf World* and *Golf* magazine, to help Jones translate his instructional articles written between 1927 and 1935 into a manuscript. *Bobby Jones on Golf*, which would ultimately sell more than twenty-five thousand copies, was released two years later. In 1969, two years before his death, Jones published his final book, *Bobby Jones on the Basic Golf Swing*.

Five days before his retirement in 1930, Jones signed a contract with Warner Brothers to make *How I Play Golf*, a series of instructional shorts that were filmed in 1931 at Lakeside Golf Club and featured actors such as James Cagney, Lionel Barrymore, and Loretta Young. The shorts were shown in more than six thousand theaters, and it is estimated that more than 25 million people saw them during the Depression. A second series, *How to Break 90,* was filmed in 1933. The actors and actresses who appeared in the film did so without pay, and director George Marshall recalled, "We had a wonderful time. All the stars were eager to take part. It was a privilege to have Jones work on their game." Marshall hired Keeler to help write the scripts and to announce at the end of each reel: "Watch for the next episode of Bobby Jones' *How I Play Golf* coming soon to your theater!" At the end of the series, Jones' modesty shone through:

> I do not mean to insist that these methods are the only ones, or even that they are the best. But I do think there are certain fundamentals which are the same for all golfers, and in making my explanations I have tried to separate these fundamentals from mannerisms that might be peculiar to my own individual style. The average golfer is not interested in winning championships. The chief benefits of the game for him must be recreation and the companionship of congenial friends. But I've always thought that if the game was worth playing at all it was worth making some effort to play correctly.

Jones also helped A. G. Spalding and Brothers design a set of woods and the first matched set of irons in 1932. Price explained the role Jones played in production: "After overseeing the casting of the irons and sanding the shafts by hand himself back in Atlanta, Jones had rejected more than two hundred different clubs until he arrived at the set that satisfied him." Jones also helped to establish and design two golf courses, Augusta National Golf Club in the early thirties and Peachtree Golf Club in 1948. He remained active in the game—even though he could not play it after 1948—as a writer, mentor, committeeman for the USGA, and host of The Masters, the role for which he is probably best remembered.

Though Jones has been gone for 34 years and it has been 75 years since he completed the Grand Slam, his legacy has not faded. In fact, he is still the subject of articles, books, documentaries, and now two feature films. Historians and golf fans have long debated who was the greatest golfer of all time. Though it is difficult to choose between players such as Jones, Ben Hogan, Byron Nelson, Jack Nicklaus, and Tiger Woods because equipment, courses, and rules are constantly in flux, Jones' record, combined with his sportsmanship and overall contributions to the game, make him a likely candidate for the top position. Maybe it is best to defer to Hagen, Jones' old friend and adversary, who once said, "If I were asked to vote for the greatest golfer of all time, I'd have to mark my ballot for Bobby Jones."

Bobby Jones' Record in the Majors

Year	Event	Site	Finish
1916	U.S. Amateur	Merion Cricket Club	Lost in the third round
1919	U.S. Amateur	Oakmont Country Club	Runner-up
1920	U.S. Open	Inverness Club	Tied for eighth
1920	U.S. Amateur	Engineers Country Club	Semifinalist
1921	British Amateur	Royal Liverpool Golf Club	Defeated in fourth round
1921	British Open	Old Course, St. Andrews	Disqualified in third round
1921	U.S. Open	Columbia Country Club	Tied for fifth
1921	U.S. Amateur	St. Louis Country Club	Lost in third round
1922	U.S. Open	Skokie Country Club	Tied for second
1922	U.S. Amateur	The Country Club	Semifinalist
1923	U.S. Open	Inwood Country Club	Winner
1923	U.S. Amateur	Flossmoor Country Club	Defeated in second round
1924	U.S. Open	Oakland Hills Country Club	Runner-up
1924	U.S. Amateur	Merion Cricket Club	Winner
1925	U.S. Open	Worcester Country Club	Runner-up
1925	U.S. Amateur	Oakmont Country Club	Winner
1926	British Amateur	Muirfield Golf Club	Defeated in sixth round
1926	British Open	Royal Lytham and St. Anne's	Winner
1926	U.S. Open	Scioto Country Club	Winner
1926	U.S. Amateur	Baltusrol Golf Club	Runner-up
1927	U.S. Open	Oakmont Country Club	Tied for eleventh
1927	British Open	Old Course, St. Andrews	Winner
1927	U.S. Amateur	Minikahda Club	Winner
1928	U.S. Open	Olympia Fields Country Club	Runner-up
1928	U.S. Amateur	Brae Burn Country Club	Winner
1929	U.S. Open	Winged Foot Golf Club	Winner
1929	U.S. Amateur	Del Monte Golf and Country Club	Defeated in first round
1930	British Amateur	Old Course, St. Andrews	Winner
1930	British Open	Royal Liverpool Golf Club	Winner
1930	U.S. Open	Interlachen Country Club	Winner
1930	U.S. Amateur	Merion Cricket Club	Winner

~2~

Bobby Jones
and the Walker
Cup Matches

> *"No man has ever had golf under his thumb. No man ever will have golf under his thumb. The game is greater than the man. Golf is like the game of life. No man ever will be its master."*
>
> —O. B. KEELER

THE FIRST WALKER CUP MATCH between the best amateur golfers in the United States and Great Britain was held on August 28–29, 1922, at the National Golf Links of America. The competition was intended to be an annual event, but the cost of transatlantic travel in the early years was prohibitive, and both teams required financial assistance. The USGA funded the American team, while the British team often solicited financial support from golf clubs. To remedy the situation, in 1924 both the USGA and the Royal and Ancient Golf Club of St. Andrews (R&A) determined that an alternate-year format would be more financially viable. The matches have only been interrupted once, for World War II. The last prewar match was played in June 1938, and play was not resumed until May 1947. Today, Walker Cup matches are played in odd-numbered years and are always scheduled before or after the British or the U.S. Amateurs.

A lifelong amateur, Bobby Jones considered his play in the Walker Cup as some of the most satisfying of his career. From 1922 to 1930, he defeated all his opponents in Walker Cup singles matches by such scores as 13 and 12 over T. Philip Perkins in 1928, and 12 and 11 over Cyril Tolley in 1926. Those two matches still hold the record for the largest winning margins in the singles matches, tied with Marvin H. Ward, who beat J. J. F. Pennick, 12 and 11, in 1938. Even today, Jones holds the record for the highest winning percentage in the singles matches, a perfect record (1.000), followed by William C. Campbell (.938) and Phil Mickelson (.875). In sum, Jones lost only one foursome match, in 1924, when he and his partner, William C. Fownes Jr., lost by one hole to Michael Scott and Robert Scott Jr. The record puts Jones in fourth place for the highest winning percentage in foursomes behind Max R. Marston, William J. Patton, and Jess W. Sweetser, and in fourth place for most victories in combined play.

The USGA named the Walker Cup for George Herbert Walker, president of the United States Golf Association in 1920. Walker, the maternal grandfather of George Bush, the 41st president of the United States, was once described as "a devoted patron, a fine sportsman, and a great gentleman." According to Walker, "the competition was begun in the wake of World War I with a view to stimulating golf interest on both sides of the Atlantic. It was born in an era of dawning internationalism and grew, at least in part, out of two international matches between Canada and the United States." The informal matches with Canada in 1919

George Herbert Walker donated the Walker Cup to the USGA.
Photo courtesy of the USGA.

and 1920 inspired Walker to create a formal competition between American and international amateur golfers.

For the first international match, in 1919, Canada invited the USGA to send an amateur team north to compete against the best Canadian amateurs. The 10-man team, captained by Fownes, who would later become president of the USGA, included John G. Anderson, Eben M. Byers, Charles "Chick" Evans Jr., Robert A. Gardner, Jones, Oswald Kirkby, Max R. Marston, Francis D. Ouimet, George Ormiston, and Jerry Travers. On July 25, 1919, the Americans defeated the Canadians, 12–3, in foursome matches in the morning and then in singles matches in the afternoon at the Hamilton Golf and Country Club in Ontario. In September 1920, for the second international match, the USGA invited the Canadian team to come south to Engineers Country Club in Roslyn Harbor, New York, where the American team won, 10–4.

Both of the matches played an important role in the establishment of the Walker Cup, but the final inspiration came when the USGA Executive Committee made a trip to Scotland to confer with the R&A about modifying various rules in the spring of 1920. Walker returned from abroad believing that the Canadian model, now twice tested, could easily extend across the Atlantic. At an Executive Committee meeting on December 21, 1920, at the Links Club in New York, Walker proposed an international competition, and his plan was accepted. He officially donated the United States Golf Association International Challenge Trophy on May 11, 1921, and it quickly became known as the Walker Cup.

In 1921, the USGA invited all golfing nations to send teams to compete, but none accepted. Not discouraged,

The 1921 U.S. Walker Cup team during a practice match at Hoylake in 1921. From left: W. C. Fownes (captain), Bobby Jones, Paul Hunter, Fred Wright Jr., Francis Ouimet, J. Wood Platt, and Jesse Guilford. Photo courtesy of the USGA.

Fownes assembled an informal team in the spring and traveled to Royal Liverpool Golf Club in Hoylake, England, where Jones would win the second leg of the Grand Slam nine years later. The team was captained by Fownes and included Jones, Ouimet, Evans, Frederick J. Wright Jr., Jesse P. Guilford, Paul Hunter, and J. Wood Platt. In order to compete, Jones had to secure permission from Georgia Tech to complete his semester a month early. The team arrived in Liverpool two weeks before the event to practice playing on links courses. Before the start of the 1921 British Amateur, the two teams played alternate-shot foursomes in the morning, and the Americans won them all. In the afternoon, the Americans took five of the eight singles matches to win 9–3.

At the outset, any country that might care to challenge the United States could enter the Walker Cup, but only Great Britain did so. The event soon became an annual celebration of the friendship between the R&A and the USGA. The teams competing for the Walker Cup are comprised of 10 golfers each, selected by the R&A and the USGA. It has since become a competition between the best male amateur golfers from the United States, Great Britain, and Ireland.

According to Gordon G. Simmonds in *The Walker Cup, 1922–1999: Golf's Finest Contest*, the R&A influenced the format of the competition. The combination of foursome and singles matches was a common format for

"Golf is the one game I know which becomes more and more difficult the longer one plays it."

—BOBBY JONES

competitions at clubs in the United Kingdom and became the model for the Walker Cup. The initial competitions were a combination of a series of foursomes on 36 holes, where two players of one side alternate strokes with one

Cyril Tolley, once called "the greatest personality in British golf," and Chick Evans Jr. putting in 1921 on the 9th green.
Photo courtesy of the USGA.

The 1922 American and British Walker Cup teams. Photo courtesy of the USGA.

ball, and one series of eight singles matches on 36 holes. In *Golf Is My Game*, Jones celebrated the virtue of foursome matches and explained that "[t]he effectiveness of a partnership in foursome play depends in large measure upon the degree of understanding between the partners." In 1963, both the foursomes and singles matches were shortened to 18 holes. In 1971, a halved match, which previously did not count, offered each team half a point.

Over the years, the Walker Cup matches have attracted the world's best amateurs, including William C. Campbell, Jones, Jack Nicklaus, Ouimet, Tolley, Roger Wethered, and Tiger Woods.

In 1922, at the age of 20, Jones, with three Southern Amateur Championships to his name, played in the first official Walker Cup. In the early years, the competition was compared to the Davis Cup in tennis. In August, in

Bobby Jones (left) and Roger Wethered at the 1922 Walker Cup.
Photo courtesy of the USGA.

advance of the matches, Innis Brown of *The American Golfer* reported: "As these lines are written the athletic sons of those two hale and hearty old gentleman of sport, John Bull and Uncle Sam, are furbishing their drivers and polishing their niblicks in anticipation of the first staging of another international tilt at sports that promises in time to become one of the big annual contests for world team supremacy."

National Golf Links was founded in 1908, and the course, designed by Charles Blair MacDonald, opened the following year. The USGA and the R&A briefly discussed alternating the Walker Cup between the National and the Old Course at St. Andrews, but the idea was finally vetoed in favor of rotating venues. The American captain for the first match was Fownes, and his team was comprised of Evans, Gardner, Guilford, Jones, Marston, Ouimet, and Sweetser. Rudolph E. Knepper was on the American team as well, but he did not play. On the British side, Robert Harris was captain. His players were Tolley, Wethered, Colin C. Aylmer, C. V. L. Hooman, Willie B. Torrance, John Caven, and W. Willis Mackenzie. The British Amateur champion, Ernest Holderness, was unable to participate because his work in the civil service conflicted with the dates. When Harris became ill with tonsillitis, Bernard Darwin, the 46-year-old golf writer for *The Times* of London who was reporting on the matches, was asked to compete in his place and serve as playing captain.

On the first day, in front of a crowd estimated at two thousand and in the midst of a terrible heat wave, the American team won three of the four foursomes. Jones teamed with Sweetser to beat Torrance and Hooman, 3

The 1922 U.S. Walker Cup team; Jones is on the far left. Photo courtesy of the USGA.

and 2. The next day, the Americans won five of the eight singles matches for an overall win of 8–4. For his individual match, Jones beat Wethered, 3 and 2. One match, between Sweetser and Hooman, went into extra holes for the first and only time in Walker Cup history. Hooman emerged victorious, and since that time, tied matches have not been played out.

USGA president Fritz Byers presented the Walker Cup to Fownes, and after a banquet that evening hosted by MacDonald, the members of both teams made their way to the Country Club in Brookline, Massachusetts, to compete in the U.S. Amateur. From September 2–6, 161 players vied for the amateur crown. The American Walker Cup team dominated the field. Sweetser, Jones, Evans,

From left: Cyril Tolley, Jess Sweetser, Francis Ouimet, and Roger Wethered at the 1923 Walker Cup match.
Photo courtesy of the USGA.

and Knepper competed in the semifinals. Only two British Walker Cup team members, Tolley and Torrance, competed. Knepper defeated them both: Torrance in the first match and Tolley in the third. In the semifinals, Jones eventually lost, 8 and 7, to Sweetser, who went on in the finals to defeat Evans, 3 and 2, to capture the title.

Jones did not compete in the second Walker Cup matches, held May 18–19, 1923, at the Old Course in St.

Andrews because it conflicted with his final exam schedule at Harvard. The team won, 6 to 5. He did, however, join the team in 1924 when the matches came to the Garden City Golf Club in New York, which was designed in 1899 by Devereau Emmet. Gardner captained the American team, comprised of Jones, Evans, Ouimet, Fownes, Harrison R. Johnston, Dr. Oscar F. Willing, Guilford, Marston, and Sweetser. Only three members of the British team—Tolley, William Murray, and William Hope—had ever played in the event. Jones teamed with Fownes for his only defeat in the Walker Cup. They lost on the 36th hole to two Scottish players, Michael Scott and Robert Scott Jr. In his singles competition, Jones won over Major Charles O. Hezlet. The Americans won the cup, 9 to 3. After the 1924 matches, the R&A and USGA elected to hold them every other year to limit the financial strain on the players and to avoid exhausting interest in the event.

In covering the 1924 competition, Grantland Rice reported:

> American golf is still somewhat stronger than British golf. If a number of matches were played the British would have a hard time finding a team quite as strong as Jones, Marston, Sweetser, Evans, Ouimet, Gardner, Guilford, Willing, Fownes, and Johnston. Yet it is easy to say that a somewhat weaker British team made a gallant fight against heavy odds over one of the hardest courses in the world—the Garden City Golf Club—where a score of 75 is an exceptional round.

Rice also observed that the American team dominated the foursomes competition, a format that was not popular in the United States. Despite the British players' partiality to the format, Great Britain and Ireland would not win the matches until 1938.

On May 5, 1926, the American Walker Cup team sailed for Great Britain aboard the RMS *Aquitania*. The team, captained by Gardner, included Jones, Sweetser, Guilford, Ouimet, Watts Gunn, and Roland MacKenzie, who was still a teenager. In fact, half the team members were under 22.

From left: captains Cyril Tolley and Robert A. Gardner before the 1924 Walker Cup. Photo courtesy of the USGA.

Only three, Ouimet, Guilford, and Gardner were over 30. But, as *The American Golfer* reported, "The American team selected is one of the strongest ever gathered. Youth or no youth, it can play a lot of golf and it will be a determined array. At least six of the eight have had their full share of experience and it will be doubly interesting to see how they fare in the British Amateur championship."

On the Old Course, Jones played in his third Walker Cup competition. Reporting on the team's trip across the Atlantic, O. B. Keeler recounted that the players hit balls into the ocean or off a device that attached the ball to a string to practice. Upon arrival, various members of the team played in the Royal St. George's Champion Grand Challenge Cup and a one-day exhibition against the

"To the finish of my golfing days I encountered golfing emotions which could not be endured with the club still in my hands."

—BOBBY JONES

Oxford and Cambridge Golfing Society at Rye Golf Club. Jones and the others then traveled to Muirfield Golf Club for the British Amateur, where Jones lost in the quarterfinals to a young player from Glasgow, Scotland, named

The 1924 British Walker Cup team. Jones defeated Major Charles O. Hezlet (fourth from left) in the singles matches.
Photo courtesy of the USGA.

From left: Jesse Sweetser, Robert Gardner, George Von Elm, and Roland Mackenzie of the 1926 United States Walker Cup team. Photo courtesy of the USGA.

Andrew Jamieson. Jones' caddie, Jack McIntyre, took the loss harder than the golfer did, and reportedly cried at the defeat. Sweetser, battling pneumonia, became the first American-born golfer to win the event.

The American team then traveled from Muirfield to St. Andrews for the Walker Cup. A few days before the start of the event, Jones visited the factory of Tom Stewart, a noted club maker, to see if he could replace the set of clubs he lost in a fire that destroyed the club-

house at East Lake in 1925. Stewart provided Jones with clubheads at a cost of $1.25 apiece. Jones had them fitted with shafts upon his return home. The Americans then set out to face the British team, comprised of Tolley, Holderness, Wethered, Hezlet, Harris, W. G. E. Brownlow, Edward F. Storey, and Jamieson. In comparing the two teams, Darwin observed of the British team, "Youth indeed does not figure very largely in the list—I wish there was more of it, but it is of no use to choose a man

The 1926 British Walker Cup team. Robert Harris, the captain, is seated in the center. Photo courtesy of the USGA.

merely because he is young and not because he is good." He went on to claim, "All I can say at present is that we shall have a better team than we did last time at St. Andrews; whether it will be good enough is another question." Unfortunately, it was not.

On June 2, the first day of the 1926 Walker Cup, Jones was paired with Gunn, his fellow club member at the Atlanta Athletic Club, and they beat Tolley and

Jamieson, 4 and 3. In his individual match, Jones defeated Tolley, 12 and 11. For the fourth time in four tries, the Americans won, this time by a margin of 6 to 5. Brown later reported in *The American Golfer*:

There was no doubt that the right side won. It was a victory for a younger, stronger, fitter side, and especially a victory for a sounder method of playing

Bobby Jones driving at the 1926 Walker Cup matches. Photo courtesy of the USGA.

The 1926 United States Walker Cup team, with Bobby Jones on the far right and Watts Gunn third from the left.
Photo courtesy of the USGA.

golf. Nobody who has watched the Americans during the last 10 days can doubt that they have been better drilled and have a surer and a better way of hitting the ball. There is a remarkable uniformity of style among them, and that style is one that stands by the player through good days and evil ones, and makes for the greatest of all golfing virtues—namely consistency.

Jones had originally booked his passage back to the United States after the Walker Cup matches, but at the last minute he canceled it to stay and play in the British Open. While the rest of the team journeyed home, Jones and George Von Elm remained in England to travel to Royal Lytham and St. Anne's Golf Club. Jones' hasty decision may have been motivated by his infamous performance at St. Andrews in 1921. Regardless of the

Members of the British Walker Cup team arriving on the SS Baltic *for the 1928 Walker Cup at Chicago Golf Club.*
Photo courtesy of the USGA.

reason, he remained and ultimately won the 1926 British Open. Later in the summer he won the U.S. Open.

In 1928, after losing the U.S. Open in June to Johnny Farrell in a playoff, Jones captained the Walker Cup team for the first time in his fourth appearance in the event. He brought an impressive team to the Chicago Golf Club for the competition on August 30 and 31, including Evans, Sweetser, Von Elm, Johnston, Ouimet, Gunn, and MacKenzie. All had played on previous Walker Cup teams. Eugene Homans and Maurice McCarthy traveled along as the two reserve players. The Chicago Golf Club, founded in 1892 by C. B. MacDonald, was one of the oldest and most prestigious clubs in America, and a few thousand spectators paid $2 to see some of the best amateurs compete. Cautiously optimistic about the American team's chances, Jones said of the competition, "We ought to win, but this is golf, and you know the old saying about golf being a humbling game."

Writer Charles Price summed up Jones' preparation:

While warming up for the Walker Cup match at the Chicago Golf Club in 1928, he established the course record at nearby Old Elm the first time he played it. A few days later, he broke the course record at Chicago. The following day, he broke that record and tied the old one the day after. A few days later, while playing in a local invitation tournament—which he won—he broke the course record at Flossmoor, despite having played the first seven holes in two over par. . . . It should be kept in mind that Jones played with hickory shafts and used a ball that was easily 30 yards shorter than today's, all over courses that were in atrocious condition by current standards, and before

numerous changes were made in the Rules, such as cleaning the ball on the green, which in themselves would make scoring measurably easier.

On the first day of the Walker Cup, the Americans won all the foursome matches. Jones and Evans won, 5 and 3, over Hezlet and Hope. On the second day, only Evans lost his singles match. Jones beat Perkins, the British Amateur champion, 13 and 12, a margin of victory that is still a record. Dr. William Tweddell, the British captain, in a moment of unguarded candor, explained what it was like to play when Jones was in the field:

I really am unable to play my game, or what I call my game, when I know that Bobby Jones is playing on the same course. . . . When he is on the course, I feel that I have no right to be out there going through the motions and playing golf. . . . Since I watched him at St. Andrews winning the British Open, I have had an inferiority complex. I feel that there is no good reason why I should play golf. Bobby Jones is a supreme artist. The rest of us, and the best of us, are no more than children, stumbling around.

The remaining members of the British team must have shared Tweddell's sentiment, as T. A. Torrance was the only member to win a point. The Americans won, 11 to 1.

The 1930 Walker Cup was scheduled more than a week before Jones won his first leg of the Grand Slam at the British Amateur at St. Andrews. A contingent from Atlanta and elsewhere, including Douglas Fairbanks, Sir Harry Lauder, Sir Joseph Duveen, and Maurice Chevalier,

The 1928 American Walker Cup team. Jones (front row, center) defeated T. Philip Perkins in the singles matches by one of the largest margins in the event's history. Photo courtesy of the USGA.

Actor Douglas Fairbanks watching 1930 American Walker Cup team member Leo Diegel practicing in Surrey, England.
Photo courtesy of the USGA.

Bobby Jones (far left) used the 1930 Walker Cup matches to prepare for the Grand Slam. Photo courtesy of the USGA.

came to see the Walker Cup. The American team was made up of Jones as captain, Johnston, Von Elm, Willing, Ouimet, George Voigt, Donald Moe, and MacKenzie, as the first reserve. The team arrived in Southampton, England, on May 6, with 10 days to prepare for the matches, to be played at the Royal St. George's Club near Sandwich, England, on May 15–16. After sightseeing,

Jones led the team to practice in London. Before the match, Jones and Johnston played a match at Sunningdale Golf Club against Edward, the Prince of Wales, and Sir Philip Sassoon. The next day the whole team traveled to Sandwich to begin practicing for the Walker Cup.

In unusually calm weather, the Americans won three of the four foursome matches on the first day. Jones was

The 1930 British Walker Cup team in Sandwich, England. Photo courtesy of the USGA.

"Despite the fact that he lived for a good half of his life in the brightest possible floodlight of public attention, he never said or did a wrong thing. Also, he managed to learn how to be not merely a good loser, which is easy, but to be a good winner, which is vastly more difficult."

—RALPH MCGILL

paired with Willing, and they won, 8 and 7. Moe was paired with MacKenzie and won, 3 and 2. In the singles, Moe won one of the greatest matches in Walker Cup history over James A. "Bill" Stout. Stout ended the morning 4 up, and was 7 up in the afternoon with just 13 holes to play. Moe took the last seven holes, winning with a birdie. Upon losing, Stout replied, "That was not golf; that was a visitation from the Lord." The Americans finished by winning seven of the eight singles matches, with Jones defeating Wethered, the British captain, 9 and 8. The final score, favoring the Americans, was 10 to 7. Over the next several weeks, Jones played in a few exhibition matches, and on May 26, with his caddie Jack McIntyre, he began his quest for the Grand Slam.

Bobby Jones during his 1930 Walker Cup singles match against Roger Wethered. Photo courtesy of the USGA.

Bobby Jones and Harrison "Jimmy" Johnston at the 1930 Walker Cup. Photo courtesy of the USGA.

Bobby Jones' Walker Cup Record

Date and Venue	Foursome Matches	Singles Matches
August 28, 1922 *National Golf Links of America*	*Robert Tyre Jones Jr. and Jess W. Sweetser defeated W. B. Torrance and C. V. L. Hooman, 3 and 2*	
August 29, 1922 *National Golf Links of America*		*Robert Tyre Jones Jr. defeated Roger Wethered, 3 and 2*
September 12, 1924 *Garden City Golf Club*	*Robert Tyre Jones Jr. and William C. Fownes Jr. lost to Michael Scott and Robert Scott Jr., 1-down*	
September 13, 1924 *Garden City Golf Club*		*Robert Tyre Jones Jr. defeated Major Charles O. Hezlet, 4 and 3*
June 2, 1926 *Old Course at St. Andrews*	*Robert Tyre Jones Jr. and Watts Gunn defeated Cyril Tolley and Andrew Jamieson, 4 and 3*	
June 3, 1926 *Old Course at St. Andrews*		*Robert Tyre Jones Jr. defeated Cyril Tolley, 2 and 11*
August 30, 1928 *Chicago Golf Club*	*Robert Tyre Jones Jr. and Charles Evans Jr. defeated Major Charles O. Hezlet and William Hope, 5 and 3*	
August 31, 1928 *Chicago Golf Club*		*Robert Tyre Jones Jr. defeated T. Philip Perkins, 13 and 12*
May 15, 1930 *Royal St. George's Golf Club*	*Robert Tyre Jones Jr. and Dr. Oscar F. Willing defeated Rex W. Hartley and T. A. Torrance, 8 and 7*	
May 16, 1930 *Royal St. George's Golf Club*		*Robert Tyre Jones Jr. defeated Roger Wethered, 9 and 8*

~3~

The Quest for
the Grand Slam

> *"He has entrenched his record safely and forever within the impregnable quadrilateral of golf."*
>
> —GEORGE TREVOR

THOUGH HE DID NOT MAKE HIS plans public at first, Bobby Jones revealed his goal of winning golf's four major championships in one year to three people: his wife, his father, and O. B. Keeler. Jones first conceived of the idea in 1926 after having lost the British Amateur for the second time. He looked forward to 1930 because the Walker Cup would be played in England, allowing him to stay abroad. The championships that comprised what Keeler eventually named the Grand Slam in 1930 were different from the four that make up today's slam. In the first decades of the 20th century, amateur golf reigned supreme and attracted some of the world's best players, notably Roger Wethered, Chick Evans, and Francis Ouimet. Two of the legs of the Grand Slam that Jones won were not even open to professional players. When Jack Nicklaus strove to match Bobby Jones' record of 13 major championship victories, he was competing in a different set of events. In addition to the U.S. Open and the British Open, Nicklaus was playing in The Masters (established by Jones and Clifford Roberts in 1934) and the PGA Championship (founded in 1916 exclusively for professional players). Only Ben Hogan and Tiger Woods have come close to achieving the modern Grand Slam. But none have done so in a single year.

Hogan, who was 18 when Jones won the Grand Slam, was once asked if the feat could ever be matched. He replied: "You never say never. But considering the times—there are so many more good players—it's improbable that any player will win all four." Tom McCollister, writing for the *Atlanta Journal-Constitution*, reflected on the significance of Jones' Grand Slam win: "Of all the single-season records of excellence in major sports, Jones' mark has stood the longest. Longer than Babe Ruth's 60 home runs, a record that lasted 34 years after he set it in 1927; longer than Joe DiMaggio's 1941 hitting streak of 56 games . . . longer than Wilt Chamberlain's 50.4 points-per-game average set in 1961–62."

From May to September of 1930, Jones embarked on an incredible quest, one that no other golfer has traveled in the sport. In *Triumphant Journey*, Richard Miller explained why it was so important:

No golfer, either professional or amateur, had won more than two major championships in one year, and only Jones himself had won both the British and the United States Opens in a single year. Way back in

1911, England's great Harold Hilton had captured both the British and United States Amateur titles, and in 1916 the remarkable Chick Evans had won the Amateur and Open championships of the United States. Such precedent would have inhibited any other golfer and brought out a dozen kinks in his swing, but Bobby Jones wasn't any other golfer.

Lloyd's of London set the odds of Jones capturing the four majors at 50-1, though there was debate at the time among sportswriters as to whether the odds were closer to 120-1.

Jones was not in great condition in January 1930. At barely 5'8", he weighed 190 pounds, and he knew the rigors ahead of him. During most major championships he lost an average of 14 pounds, often the result of vomiting bouts brought on by anxiety. In the first months of 1930, Jones played a game called Dougledyas, named for its inventor, Douglas Fairbanks. A cross between tennis and badminton, it could be played indoors and allowed Jones to build his strength and lose weight. When the weather permitted, he also traveled to Highlands Country Club in North Carolina, a course his father had helped to establish and one where Jones frequently played during the summer months, to practice golf and play tennis away from the adoring crowds. That spring, Jones played in the mountains with Chick Ridley and John Grant, two noted Atlanta amateurs, as well as baseball player Ty Cobb. In the first two weeks of February, Jones began playing golf several times each week. On February 15, he shot a 63 at East Lake and seemed poised to begin the season. By March, he weighed 165 pounds and was in fine condition.

To prepare himself for the first leg of what would become the Grand Slam, Jones entered two regional events in the spring. This was an important decision, as he usually played an average of six tournaments per year. He strongly believed, though, that to capture all four majors, he must expand that schedule. He finished second at the Savannah Open, played at the Savannah Golf Club, one stroke behind Horton Smith, who would go on to win the first Masters in 1934. Unable to share in the $3,000 purse, Jones was given a 12-gauge, double-barreled shotgun as the low amateur. A few weeks after he turned 28, Jones easily won the Southeastern Open, played at Augusta Country Club and the Forrest Hills–Ricker course from March 31 to April 1, with a 13-shot victory margin over Smith. Watching him play, Bobby Cruickshank, who was 29 strokes behind Jones, said to Keeler, "Bob is just too good. His play in this tournament is the finest thing I have ever seen, and do you want a prediction? Here's one. He's going to win the British Amateur and British Open, and then he's coming back here to win the National Open and National Amateur. They'll never stop him this year." Betting on his prediction, Cruickshank wagered $500 with a bookmaker in Great Britain and eventually won $60,000. Jones would later say of the Southeastern Open, "That's where I played my finest golf of 1930."

Jones and his wife, Keeler, John G. Jackson of the USGA, members of the Walker Cup team, and other friends, including Douglas Fairbanks, left New York on April 30, 1930, for England aboard the RMS *Mauretania* to participate in the Walker Cup matches, the British Amateur, and the British Open. The travel to and from England was paid for by the USGA because Jones was a

From left: Bobby Jones, George Von Elm, and Douglas Fairbanks relaxing during the British Amateur in 1930.
Photo courtesy of the USGA.

member of the Walker Cup team. On May 15–16 at the Royal St. George's Golf Club in Sandwich, England, Jones captained the team to victory. Though he was the best golfer in the world, as captain he gave the number one position to Harrison Johnston, the reigning U.S. Amateur champion. For the sixth time in six attempts, the United States team was victorious. With the exception of 1923, when he was studying at Harvard, Jones

played on every Walker Cup team from 1922 to 1930. A few days later, Jones played in a 36-hole exhibition match, *Golf Illustrated*'s Gold Vase, at Sunningdale Golf Club, which he won with a 75 and a 68 for a total of 143 on May 19. Jones then traveled to St. Andrews for the British Amateur—the only major championship he had not won and the one he would later call "the most important tournament of my life."

On May 26, 1930, Jones began his third attempt to capture the British Amateur. Photo courtesy of the USGA.

At St. Andrews, Jones faced his toughest test: eight 18-hole matches and one 36-hole match. The shorter matches were his least favorite competitive format because Jones believed that any player could play well for 18 holes. He always believed that 36 holes was a better measure of a golfer's true ability. Twenty-four Americans, including the entire American Walker Cup team, were included in the field of 172 competitors for the British Amateur. Donald Moe, one of the Walker Cup team members from Portland, Oregon, recalled the condition of the course, "To our surprise we found St. Andrews hard and dry due to a long winter, which turned into a hot summer in mid-May, a most unusual situation because the golf course is the beneficiary of the frequent squalls from the North Sea." To adjust to the conditions, Moe recalled, the American players "looked for balls that had been in the water for some time" because they "required a fairly dead ball for control."

Before a gallery of twenty thousand fans, Jones won seven straight 18-hole matches, as he had earned a bye in the first round, and defeated Roger Wethered in the final 36-hole match, 7 and 6. During the five competition days, Jones only carded two double bogeys. Astonished by Jones' performance, F. C. Stevens of Los Angeles, whose son was in the field, joked, "They ought to burn him at the stake. He's a witch." Elated by his victory, Jones turned to Keeler to say, "O. B., honestly, I don't care what happens now. I'd rather have won this tournament than anything else in golf. I'm satisfied." Back home in Atlanta, Frank Ball, the Atlanta Athletic Club's head professional at the East Lake course, upon hearing the good news, threw his mashie in the lake in a fit of joy.

Bobby Jones (left) defeated George Voigt in the semifinals of the British Amateur. Photo courtesy of the USGA.

Bobby Jones during the fourth round of the British Amateur. Photo courtesy of the USGA.

After a brief holiday in Paris with his wife, Jones traveled to the Royal Liverpool Golf Club in Hoylake, England, for the British Open. His win at Hoylake would make him the first player since John Ball in 1890 to win both British events. Worried about his driving and putting, Jones qualified with a 73 at Hoylake and a 77 at Wallasey Golf Club for a 150, nine strokes behind medalist Archie Compston and in 20th place. If Jones played his best golf at the Southeastern Open earlier in the spring, he played his worst at the British Open. Keeler later reflected, "He got more golf out of a worse game than he has ever managed before in an important competition." Jones agreed, confessing to Keeler, "I simply don't know where the darned ball is going when I hit it."

In the first two rounds he shot a 70 and a 72 to take a 1-stroke lead. But in the third round, his 74 moved him to second behind Compston, who carded a 68. In the final round, Jones shot a 75, and Compston, who bogeyed the 1st hole in the afternoon, carded an 82. Jones had to wait for more than an hour for Macdonald Smith and Leo Diegel to finish their rounds. Diegel's chances faded on the 16th hole when he took a bogey. Smith came to the final hole needing to hole his approach shot to tie Jones. Instead, it bounced on the green and ran past the cup. Jones had won. *The Times* in London declared it a "triumph of courage and putting." His score of 291 was 10 strokes better than Walter Hagen's score when he won the British Open at Hoylake in 1924. During each evening of the event, Keeler summarized Jones' play in 15-minute segments, and NBC broadcast them on both sides of the Atlantic.

With his third British Open title and after playing in an exhibition match with James Braid, Harry Vardon, and

After winning the 1930 British Amateur, Jones declared, "I have been very lucky. The breaks were mine." Photo courtesy of the USGA.

Crowds at the 1930 British Open. Photo courtesy of the USGA.

Ted Ray, Jones and his family returned to America on board the SS *Europa*, arriving in New York City on July 2, 1930. The returning champion was escorted to Battery Park aboard a tug boat called *Macom*. Mayor Jimmy Walker and Joseph Johnson, former commissioner of Public Works, accompanied Jones on the city's tug boat that was decorated with a banner that read "Welcome to the World's Champion Golfer." Two hundred and fifty Atlantans, who had come to New York aboard a train named the "Bobby Jones Special," sailed out to greet him aboard the *Mandalay*. For becoming the first golfer in 40 years and the first American golfer to win both British tournaments in a single year, New York rewarded Jones with a second ticker-tape parade up Broadway. At 4:00 in the afternoon, 70 mounted policeman led a motorcade from Battery Park up Broadway, accompanied by the Sanitation Department band.

At City Hall Plaza, Jones was toasted by Walker, who began his remarks, "Here you are, the greatest golfer in the world, being introduced by the worst one." Walker concluded that the titles Jones had amassed, "never will be won by a finer gentleman or a better sportsman." Jones replied, "I am overcome by the kind things you have said and the tremendous welcome accorded me. I have not experienced anything like this before. When I came up Broadway I tried to figure out the reason for it. Ordinarily when I intend to speak I make up my speech as the other fellow goes along, but I was cut off my game this time. All I can say is that I am overwhelmed by the welcome I have received from the people of the city of New York and the people of Atlanta, Georgia. I have never been so impressed." After Major John S. Cohen, the editor of the

Jones putting during the 1930 U.S. Open at Interlachen. Photo courtesy of the USGA.

Clara and Bobby Jones III on June 22, 1930, after the British Open.
Photo courtesy of the Jones family.

Atlanta Journal, called for "three cheers for Jimmy Walker," Jones and his entourage stepped into waiting cars to depart for a formal dinner. One spectator, unaware of what was going on, asked a nearby police officer, "What's the parade for?" The officer replied, "Oh, for some Goddamn golf player!"

Several other notable athletes and public figures had enjoyed ticker-tape parades in their honor. Gertrude Ederle, who in 1926 became the first woman to swim the English Channel, was given one, as was Charles Lindbergh, who in 1927 successfully completed

Jones' second ticker tape parade came two weeks after a similar parade for Admiral Richard E. Byrd. Photo courtesy of the Jones family.

the first flight across the Atlantic. Until John Glenn's second trip into space in 1998, Jones was the only person ever given two ticker-tape parades in New York. After Jones won the two British events, Keeler, writing for the *Atlanta Journal*, began calling the quest the "Grand Slam."

That evening, the Vanderbilt Hotel hosted 400 guests, including Findley Douglas of the USGA and Charles Blair MacDonald, the winner of the first U.S. Amateur in 1895. The next day, Jones, his parents, Cyril Tolley, and Keeler

boarded the train for Minneapolis, Minnesota. His wife, Mary, returned to Atlanta to help care for their children, Clara and Bob III.

Two weeks after his victory in Hoylake, Jones won the U.S. Open, the third leg of the Grand Slam, at Interlachen Country Club in Minnesota, a 6,672-yard course, during a stifling heat wave. While waiting to tee off one day, a spectator asked Jones if he was aware that the temperature was 110 degrees in the shade. Jones replied, "Well, it's a good thing we don't have to play in

Jones posing with the British Open, British Amateur, and U.S. Open trophies prior to the last leg of the Grand Slam.
Photo courtesy of the USGA.

the shade, isn't it?" Against a field of 143 players, Jones, with his caddie Donovan Dale, opened with a 71, one stroke behind Tommy Armour and Macdonald Smith. The heat was so intense that Jim Barnes carried an umbrella, Armour rubbed his face with ice before each shot, and Cyril Tolley lost nine pounds on the first day.

On the 9th hole of the second round, Jones hit what was arguably the most bizarre shot of the tournament. Distracted by two young girls that he saw out of the corner

moment, "As I stepped up to the putt, I was quivering in every muscle." Jones finished with a 75 and a final score of 287, one stroke off the U.S. Open record. He had to wait an hour to learn that he had defeated Macdonald Smith by two strokes. Horton Smith, the third-place finisher, said at the trophy ceremony, "We've all tried hard to corner the elusive Mr. Jones, but haven't succeeded. We certainly would like to beat him better than anything else in the world, but we haven't had any experience in doing

"Perhaps the fighters of old days were better, the football players more ferocious, the winters colder and the snow deeper, but there was never a golfer the equal of Jones in five centuries of wild whacking about the links."

—JOHN KIERNAN

of his eye, Jones topped his ball, which skipped across the surface of the pond. What was later erroneously called the "lily pad shot," ended up a short pitch away from the green, and Jones birdied the hole with a 4. He finished the back nine with a 39. At the end of the second round, he was tied with Harry Cooper and Charles Lacey for second place behind Horton Smith, who had a 142. In the third round, calling upon what Richard Miller termed a "perfect fusion of his mental and physical powers," Jones finished with six birdies, 10 pars, and two bogeys for a 68. In the tumultuous final round, Jones came to the final hole leading by a single stroke. Later he described the final

it." Jones won his fourth U.S. Open and tied a record set by Willie Anderson. In nine consecutive attempts, Jones finished first four times and second four times.

Atlanta welcomed Jones home with another parade, and Atlanta Mayor I. N. Ragsdale presented Jones with a gold key to the city as a "symbol of affection of his friends and neighbors." The *Atlanta Constitution* reported that 125,000 fans turned out to see Jones and that it appeared to be "snowing along Peachtree Street" because the confetti was so thick. His daughter, Clara, who was five, recalled the event: "I remember us going out to flag the train down at the Emory station because Dad didn't want to come into

The Jones family during the parade in Atlanta after the 1930 U.S. Open. Photo courtesy of the Jones family.

the downtown station. We got out and waved handkerchiefs at the train, and there was some silly picture in the newspaper of us doing that. But it was the parade I'll always remember. I'll never forget riding in that convertible with the leather seats in the heat of the summer. It was unbearable. It was one of the most horrible days."

After Jones won the U.S. Open at Interlachen, members of the press began urging Jones to reveal what he was going to do when he retired. In the locker room after the win in July 1930, one reporter asked Jones again. Jones turned to Keeler and said, "You'd better tell them, O. B.—you know." Keeler stood and recited from memory the lines of a poem by Hilaire Belloc:

If I ever become a rich man,
Or if I ever grow to be old,
I will build a house with a deep thatch
To shelter me from the cold.
I will hold my house in the high woods
Within a walk of the sea,
And the men that were boys when I was a boy
Shall sit and drink with me.

Jones had one championship left.

The road to Merion and the U.S. Amateur was probably the hardest one Jones would travel. A few weeks after winning at Interlachen, disaster seemed to stalk him. Late in July, Jones was nearly hit by a car while walking on Carnegie Way on the way to a business lunch at the Atlanta Athletic Club's downtown facility. On September 11, Jones visited several doctors because he was suffering from acute pains in his abdomen.

> *"In 1930 Americans viewed Merion as more than a golf course, and the U.S. Amateur as more than a golf tournament. It was a battleground of hope for a people experiencing the dread of the Depression. Jones held the promise of man fulfilling his greatest potential against staggering odds."*
>
> —RICHARD MILLER

Wrongly diagnosed as appendicitis, it was finally determined that the pains were the result of stress. Though the doctor discouraged him from competing at Merion, Jones refused and requested medication to help him manage the pain and anxiety. The doctor, so concerned about Jones' condition, insisted upon accompanying him to Pennsylvania. Five days before the Amateur Jones attended a reception at the White House with Herbert Hoover and played in an exhibition match with Horton Smith at the Columbia Country Club in Chevy Chase, Maryland. The exhibition helped to raise money for an assistant club professional who had been severely injured in a car accident. Jones then made his way to Merion.

Jones at Merion Golf Club in 1930. Photo courtesy of the USGA.

Jones played the last leg of the Grand Slam at the same place where he played in his first major championship in 1916 at the age of 14—Merion Cricket Club (now Merion Golf Club) in Ardmore, outside of Philadelphia, Pennsylvania. There was intense international interest about whether Jones could complete an unprecedented sweep of golf's four majors. His performance, against the 168 qualifiers, was front-page news, and more than 2 million words were devoted to covering the championship in newspapers around the globe that week. In *Triumphant Journey,* Miller explained that the editor of the *Philadelphia Evening Bulletin* assigned 16 writers and photographers to cover the championship, some of whom knew nothing about golf. For 15 minutes every evening, Keeler provided a synopsis of the day's play to radio listeners who tuned into NBC.

To brace himself for what lay ahead, Jones settled into a warm bath at the Barclay Hotel with a glass of corn whiskey, his favorite drink brought from Atlanta. On Wednesday of the practice rounds, attended by more than four thousand spectators, Jones struggled with his putting and shot a 73. His 19-year-old caddie, Howard Rexford, was selected from a pool of nearly 350 applicants to carry Jones' bag, which was weighed down by 18 clubs. The rule limiting the number of clubs in a player's bag to 14 was not adopted by the USGA until 1938. One sportswriter estimated that Rexford, who was paid $175 for the week, carried that bag more than 60 miles. Before the second practice round on Thursday, Jones was made an honorary member of the Penn Athletic Club, one of only five other Americans to have been so honored. That afternoon he shot a 78 in the practice round and left the course in frustration.

To help Jones escape the crowds and concentrate on his game, Jess Sweetser, a close friend and fellow competitor, suggested that they play at Pine Valley Golf Club in Clementon, New Jersey. After a more relaxed round, Jones, an avid baseball fan, spent the afternoon with Sweetser watching the St. Louis Cardinals beat the Phillies. The brief pause helped prepare him for the upcoming competition.

proved to be the turning point of the match. Both Jones and Somerville had tough putts; Jones made his, took a 2-up lead, and ultimately won, 5 and 4. After a light lunch, Jones faced Hoblitzel. Neither golfer played well, and Jones won again, 5 and 4. The last three rounds were played over 36 holes, a format Jones preferred. He won the quarterfinals, 6 and 5, over Fay Coleman. In the semifinal on September

> *"It is no accident that Mr. Robert T. Jones is almost the only champion in any branch of sport who is genuinely popular with those who play against him."*
>
> —JOHN R. TUNIS

The day before the two qualifying rounds, Jones played yet another practice round to accommodate USGA president Findley Douglas, who wanted to give the galleries as much exposure to Jones as possible. He shot a 69. The next morning, September 22, 1930, Jones began the first qualifying round at 9:18 in the morning. Three hours later, he finished the round 1 under par for a 69 and was leading the field. The next day, he shot a 73, which gave him a total of 142 and the medal for the lowest score in qualifying. It was the sixth time that Jones was either medalist or comedalist in the Amateur.

Jones won the first two 18-hole matches against two Canadian golfers, Charles Ross "Sandy" Somerville and Fred Hoblitzel. Though not widely known in the United States, Somerville was a star in Canada and was good at maintaining his composure under pressure. The 7th hole

26, Jones defeated his old friend, Jess Sweetser, 9 and 8. In the other semifinal match, Charlie Seaver, the father of baseball player Tom Seaver, and Eugene Homans battled to get to the final bracket. Homans, who beat Seaver 1-up, was a 22-year-old player from New Jersey who had a short drive, but a good short game.

On September 27, a cool fall day in Pennsylvania, Jones faced Homans in the finals at 9:15 in the morning. An hour before their tee time, the crowd was estimated at nine thousand people. Homans was clearly distracted by being the last obstacle Jones faced to win the Grand Slam, and did not card a par for the first five holes. At the end of 18, Jones was 7-up. By the afternoon, the gallery had doubled to eighteen thousand and Jones, Homans, and their caddies had to be protected by U.S. Marines that had been hired to control the crowds. Homans seemed to find

Bobby Jones during his final match at the U.S. Amateur in 1930 against Eugene Homans. Photo courtesy of the USGA.

a second wind, but he could not catch Jones. On the 11th hole of the afternoon (and the 29th hole of the match), Homans missed a 25-foot putt and extended his hand to concede the match to Jones before his ball stopped rolling, giving Jones an 8-and-7 victory. When Ernest Rogers, a reporter for the *Atlanta Journal*, called Mary

Jones to tell her that her husband had won, she replied, "That's grand. After the morning round, I thought he would win, but it is a comfort to know it's all over." Thirty years later, the members at Merion placed a granite monument in front of the 11th green to commemorate the spot upon which he completed the Grand Slam.

Eighteen thousand spectators were at Merion when Jones beat Homans, 8 and 7, to win the Grand Slam. Photo courtesy of the USGA.

When Jones finally reached the table by the first tee to accept the Havermeyer Trophy, named for the first president of the USGA, he was exhausted and the crowd was in a frenzy. Jones' name would be engraved on the trophy for a record fifth time. In his acceptance speech, he said, "I expect to continue to play golf, but just when and where I cannot say now. I have no definite plans either to retire or as to when and where I may continue in competitions. I might play next year or lay off in 1932. I might stay out of the battle next season and feel like another tournament the following year. That's all I can say about it now." Privately, Jones was elated that he could now "play golf for the fun of it."

Joe Dey, then a sportswriter in Philadelphia, recalled the event in 1930: "I saw every shot, and I haven't seen anyone since as dominant as Jones was in that Amateur. None of his matches went past the 14th hole. He cruised along. Considering the pressure and the crowds—you have to remember in those days the fairways weren't roped—it was a remarkable performance by a remarkable player." In *Triumphant Journey*, Richard Miller summarized Jones' incredible feat: "In total, Jones had actually played only 20 days of championship golf over four months; but on half those days, he had been scheduled to play 36 holes. He had played 475 holes of golf. In the British and U.S. Opens, at stroke play, he had averaged 72.5 strokes. At Merion, Jones played 152 holes, in approximately 17 strokes over par, or more precisely four over even fours." To attest to Jones' drawing power, the total gate receipts for the Amateur were $55,319. In comparison, the 1964 U.S. Amateur made $17,261.

Journalists searched for words to adequately describe the accomplishment. *The New York Times* writer William D. Richardson declared, "It was the most triumphant journey that any man has ever travelled in sport." George Trevor of the *New York Sun* called the feat the "impregnable quadrilateral of golf." But it was Keeler's term, *Grand Slam*, which he borrowed from contract bridge and first used after the British Open, that eventually stuck. The feat still stands as among the most remarkable in all of golf. Al Laney reported in the *New York Herald Tribune*, "The cumulative excitement of that summer-long quest, participated in by millions on both sides of the Atlantic, has no parallel in the history of sport." In 1944, American sportswriters named it the "outstanding sports achievement of all time." In 1950,

the Associated Press voted it "the supreme athletic achievement of this century."

Jones' reflection on his fourth and final win revealed the strain of competition and foreshadowed his retirement: "I felt the wonderful feeling of release from tension and relaxation that I had wanted so badly for so long a time. I wasn't quite certain what had happened or what I had done. I only knew that I had completed a period of most strenuous effort and that at this point, nothing more remained to be done, and that once I had completed this particular project, at least, there could never at any time in the future be anything else to do."

Writing for the *Atlanta Journal-Constitution*, Tom McCollister put Jones' record in perspective:

> From 1923 to 1930, Jones won 13 major national titles in the U.S. and Great Britain, 62 percent of the championships he entered. In the last 11 British and U.S. Opens in which he played, he finished no worse than second in 10, winning seven times. . . . In his 13 years in major championship competition, he was a student, high school or college, in nine of them. He played in only 52 tournaments in that span, an average of four a year, and won 23.

On November 17, 1930, at the age of 28 and 52 days after he won the last leg of the Grand Slam, Bobby Jones surprised his fans and competitors by announcing his retirement from tournament golf. Retirement allowed him to sign a contract with Warner Brothers and turn his attention to his family and law practice. He made his intentions clear in a letter to Herbert Ramsey, vice president of

U.S. OPEN AMERICAN AMATEUR WALKER CUP BRITISH AMATEUR BRITISH OPEN
GOLF TROPHIES of ROBERT T. JONES JR. 1930

The result of Jones' quest. Photo courtesy of the Jones family.

the USGA, who then distributed it to the press: "Fourteen years of intense tournament play in this country and abroad have given me all I wanted in the way of hard work in the game. I have reached the point where I felt that my profession required more of my time and effort, leaving golf in its proper place, as a means of obtaining recreation and enjoyment." In an editorial titled "Bobby Holes Out," *The New York Times* reflected on Jones' decision: "With dignity he quits the memorable scene upon which he nothing common did or mean."

Sportswriters and journalists of the time agreed that despite the fact that Jones beat some of the best professionals of his day and his four U.S. Open victories cost them more than $200,000 in prize money and endorsements, his retirement was still mourned. John Kiernan, writing for *The New York Times*, explained why, "He boomed the whole game of golf. He made the open championships greater events by the very fact that he was in the field. He was the greatest advertisement golf ever had."

The total prize money for the 1926 U.S. Open was $2,146. Second, it would have been beneath Jones' class. Drawing on Victorian ideals, golfers in America and Great Britain believed that true sportsmen and gentlemen should remain amateurs. Jones fully subscribed to this ideology, but the professionals loved him. Jones served as an honorary vice president of the Professional Golfers' Association of America (PGA) from 1931 until his death. In *A Golf Story*, Charles Price tells the story from one

"There are no more golfing worlds left to conquer for this 28-year-old citizen-lawyer of Atlanta, Georgia, who made his final triumph look so ridiculously easy that the wonder is he hasn't been doing this sort of thing every year since he first began to scale the height."

—ASSOCIATED PRESS, 1930

For decades historians and sportswriters speculated as to why Jones did not turn professional. In "Not My Business," an article for *Colliers* magazine in 1930, Jones explained why he elected to remain an amateur. He did not see the appeal in "night after night on Pullmans, round after round of golf played before thunderous crowds, and little possibility of enjoying home." Turning professional would not have been a wise career choice for two reasons. First, there was not much money to be made, and most professionals were widely considered what Jones called in a letter to Clifford Roberts "an uneducated club servant."

professional, Orville White, who played with Jones: "When Bob was playing down a parallel fairway, we all stopped what we were doing. You just could not play golf when you had the chance to watch him. He was just— well, like no one we had ever seen." The professionals even extended to Jones an invitation to play in the PGA Championship upon his retirement. "Should Bobby's entrance into the movies affect his amateur standing, the professionals would look forward with joy to meeting him at some future time in their own match play championship— the one world he has not conquered."

The British Amateur

The Old Course at St. Andrews, Scotland

Format: Eight 18-hole rounds of match play. The final was a 36-hole round of match play.
No qualifying round.

Round	Format	Competitor	Score
Round 1	*18 holes match play*	*Bye*	
Round 2 *Monday, May 26, 1930 (afternoon)*	*18 holes match play*	*Henry Sydney Roper*	*3 and 2*
Round 3 *Wednesday, May 28, 1930 (morning)*	*18 holes match play*	*Cowan Shankland*	*5 and 3*
Round 4 *Wednesday, May 28, 1930 (afternoon)*	*18 holes match play*	*Cyril J. H. Tolley*	*19th hole*
Round 5 *Thursday, May 29, 1930 (morning)*	*18 holes match play*	*G. O. Watt*	*7 and 6*
Round 6 *Thursday, May 29, 1930 (afternoon)*	*18 holes match play*	*Harrison R. Johnston*	*1-up*
Round 7 *Friday, May 30, 1930 (morning)*	*18 holes match play*	*Eric Fiddian*	*4 and 3*
Semifinals *Friday, May 30, 1930 (afternoon)*	*18 holes match play*	*George Voigt*	*1-up*
Finals *Saturday, May 31, 1930 (morning)*	*36 holes match play*	*Roger Wethered*	*7 and 6*

The British Open
Royal Liverpool Golf Club, Hoylake, England

Format: Two 18-hole qualifying rounds and four rounds of 18 holes of stroke play.

Round	Format	Score
Qualifying Round June 16, 1930	*18 holes stroke play*	*73 at Hoylake*
Qualifying Round June 17, 1930	*18 holes stroke play*	*77 at Wallasey*
Round 1 June 18, 1930	*18 holes stroke play*	*70*
Round 2 June 19, 1930	*18 holes stroke play*	*72*
Round 3 June 20, 1930 (morning)	*18 holes stroke play*	*74*
Round 4 June 20, 1930 (afternoon)	*18 holes stroke play*	*75*

The U.S. Open
Interlachen Country Club, Minneapolis, Minnesota

Format: Two 18-hole qualifying rounds of stroke play and four rounds of stroke play of 18 holes.

Round	Format	Score
Qualifying round	*18 holes stroke play*	*As defending champion, Jones was exempt from the qualifying round*
Qualifying round	*18 holes stroke play*	*As defending champion, Jones was exempt from the qualifying round*
Round 1 July 10, 1930	*18 holes stroke play*	*71*
Round 2 July 11, 1930	*18 holes stroke play*	*73*
Round 3 July 12, 1930 (morning)	*18 holes stroke play*	*68*
Round 4 July 12, 1930 (afternoon)	*18 holes stroke play*	*75*

The U.S. Amateur
Merion Cricket Club, Ardmore, Pennsylvania

Format: Two qualifying rounds of 18 holes of stroke play. The first two rounds of match play were 18 holes each; the last three rounds of match play were 36 holes.

Round	Format	Competitor	Score
Qualifying round *September 22, 1930*	*18 holes* *stroke play*		*69*
Qualifying round *September 23, 1930*	*18 holes* *stroke play*		*73*
Round 1 *September 24, 1930* *(morning)*	*18 holes* *match play*	*C. Ross Somerville*	*5 and 4*
Round 2 *September 24, 1930* *(afternoon)*	*18 holes* *match play*	*Fred G. Hoblitzel*	*5 and 4*
Round 3 *September 25, 1930*	*36 holes* *match play*	*Fay Coleman*	*6 and 5*
Semifinals *September 26, 1930*	*36 holes* *match play*	*Jess W. Sweetser*	*9 and 8*
Finals *September 27, 1930*	*36 holes* *match play*	*Eugene V. Homans*	*8 and 7*

~4~
The Jones
Family Album

"I knew he played golf every Sunday. But it wasn't until he returned from the Grand Slam that I knew anything spectacular was going on."

—CLARA BLACK

JONES' GRANDFATHER, ROBERT Tyre Jones Sr., the son of William Green Jones (1822–1888) and Emily F. Chaffin Jones (1825–1903), was a pious man from Canton, Georgia. He was born in 1849 and, after the Civil War, worked on the family farm near Covington, Georgia, until he was 30 years old. With $500 in his pocket, he moved to Canton in 1879 with his wife, Susan Smith Walker Jones, and six-month-old son, Robert Permedus, to establish the Jones Mercantile Company. Ten years later, in the midst of the 1893 depression, the company's profits exceeded $100,000. At the age of 50, in 1899, Jones Sr. started the Canton Textile Mills, which in 1925 made more than $1.5 million.

On September 23, 1937, Robert Tyre Jones Sr. died, leaving a sizable estate. His son was an avid sportsman, especially when it came to baseball. He was a star outfielder for three years at Mercer University and for one at the University of Georgia before being offered a contract with the team that eventually became the Brooklyn Dodgers. When his father heard about the contract he responded with disdain, "I didn't send you to college to become a professional baseball player." Robert Permedus became a lawyer instead and was admitted to the Georgia Bar. On June 1, 1900, he married Clara Merrick Thomas, the daughter of a respected judge in Auburn who had also been a captain in the Spanish-American War. In April 1901, Clara and Bob had their first child, whom they named William Bailey, after Clara's father. Three months later he died. Clara blamed the poor medical care in Canton and insisted that the family move to the larger, more cosmopolitan city of Atlanta, which had a population of ninety thousand. On March 17, 1902 at 7:35 A.M., Robert Tyre Jones Jr. was born in the Grant Mansion, a two-story Italianate house built in 1857. Early in 1907, the family moved to an apartment on West Peachtree Street, and that summer rented a house in Atlanta's East Lake suburb just as golf was becoming popular in the United States.

In Atlanta, Robert Permedus Jones, fondly known as "the Colonel," became a respected lawyer, who counted the Coca-Cola Company as one of his many clients. Always an avid athlete, he and his wife took up golf at the Atlanta Athletic Club's newly completed East Lake course. They took lessons from the club's Scottish golf professional, James Maiden, before he left to become the pro

Bobby Jones' future wife, Mary Malone, on right, with her two brothers. Photo courtesy of the USGA.

"The secret of Jones' success was the strength of the man's mind."
—BEN HOGAN

at the Nassau Country Club on Long Island, New York. James was succeeded by his brother, Stewart. Bobby Jones, or Robert, as he was called by his mother, was not allowed on the course, so he and his older friend, Frank Meador, built a makeshift course along the road near the Meador's boarding house. With a few cut-down clubs, Jones began to play the game for which he would become famous. In *Golf Is My Game*, he explained, "There was nothing very conscious or contrived about the whole process. The game was there, I liked it, and I kept on playing." Jones never had formal lessons, but learned mostly by watching Stewart Maiden play with other members at East Lake. Though father and son did not often compete against each other, in 1915, at the Atlanta Athletic Club Championship, a 13-year-old Jones faced his father in the last round and won, 4 and 3. Years later, in 1955 at the Atlanta Athletic Club's celebration dinner for the 25th anniversary of the Grand Slam, Jones remembered his father not as a competitor but as a mentor, "My father, bless him, at great personal sacrifice, made it possible for me to play in many tournaments."

Jones attended the Calhoun and Woodbury schools in Atlanta and, at the age of 16, in the spring of 1918, graduated with high marks from Tech High School. After an

When Bobby Jones passed the Georgia bar he joined the firm where his father, Robert Permedus Jones, worked.
Photo courtesy of the USGA.

active summer of playing golf, on September 24, Jones entered Georgia Tech. He majored in mechanical engineering and joined the Sigma Alpha Epsilon fraternity. Jones and Perry Adair played varsity golf for Tech, and Jones served as the captain of the Golden Tornadoes. In Tech's yearbook, *The Blueprint*, the following caption accompanied Jones' picture: "Yes, this is none other than the famous Bob of golfing fame. We can't tell you too much about him that you don't already know unless that he's a darn good student as well as a golfer, not to mention he is exceedingly popular with his fellow students." In June 1922, Jones graduated in the top third of his class and was awarded a bachelor of science degree in mechanical engineering.

In the fall, on September 25, 1922, Jones entered Harvard University to complete a second bachelor's degree in English literature. He counted among his classmates Henry Cabot Lodge and Ogden Nash. Many years later, his granddaughter, Merry Black, remembered Jones' intellect: "He read the dictionary as most would read a book, and he had a command of the English language that few possess. If he heard or read a word with which he was not familiar, by the end of the day, he knew not only what it meant, but where it came from and how it is used and anything else you might ever want to know about a word. The whole family was informed of it as well." While at Harvard, he served as the golf team's assistant manager, which often meant carrying the bourbon to tournaments, because his play at Tech made him ineligible. When later asked why he accepted the position, he replied: "How else was I going to get the crimson *H*?" He was ultimately awarded an honorary letter and voted into the Varsity Hall of Fame. He was less active in the social life at Harvard than he was at Tech, studying composition and comparative literature, and taking French and German. When he requested permission to take his final exams early to participate in the second Walker Cup, he was denied. In 1924, he completed his degree and returned to Atlanta to begin selling lots near the Whitfield Estates Golf and Country Club for the Adair Realty Company with Perry's cousin, Forrest Adair Jr. By then, Jones was a member of the Atlanta Athletic Club, Druid Hills Golf Club, and the Capital City Club. On September 28, 1926, Jones, who quickly determined that real estate was not his future, entered Emory University School of Law. While at Emory, he was made an honorary member of the Royal and Ancient Golf Club of St. Andrews.

At 8:30 P.M. on Tuesday, June 17, 1924, after a five-year courtship and a week-long series of teas, dances, and bridal parties, Bobby Jones married Mary Rice Malone on the lawn of the Malone home. The two had met several years earlier on a trolley car, and she was the sister of two of his friends at Georgia Tech, John and Matthew Malone. Born on July 24, 1902, and raised in a house on Springdale Road in Atlanta's wealthy Druid Hills neighborhood, Malone was one of three children. She was educated at Girls' High School and later Mary Washington Seminar for Girls in Atlanta. Because Mary was a devout Irish Catholic and Jones was not, the wedding could not be held in her church. Father James Horton of the Sacred Heart Church performed the marriage ceremony. Jones agreed to raise the children Catholic. The *Atlanta Constitution* later described the event as "a social event of rare beauty." Jones and Mary honeymooned at the Biltmore Forest Country Club in Asheville, North Carolina. When they returned, they lived with Jones' parents to save money while Jones joined Adair Realty, beginning his short career in real estate.

Jones managed to complete his schooling, marry, and begin raising his family all while maintaining an active competitive schedule. During his 14 years competing in national championships, he was often a student, either in high school or college. He somehow managed to keep it all in perspective, making his priorities clear, "My wife and children come first, then my profession. Finally, and never in a life by itself, came golf." Grantland Rice once wrote that while traveling to a championship, Jones "might be found with a Latin book or a calculus treatise, completely engrossed, with all thought of golf eliminated until he

Bobby Jones' mother, Clara, urged Jones' father to move from Canton, Georgia, to Atlanta. Photo courtesy of the USGA.

Bobby Jones (right) with Charles J. Hilkey, dean of Emory University Law School. Photo courtesy of Special Collections, Robert W. Woodruff Library, Emory University.

reached the scene of battle." This is even more extraordinary when one considers the toll competitive golf took on Jones. He once confessed in a 1930 *Golf Monthly* article, "People may get the impression that I find it easy to go on playing golf day after day without breaking down. But it is really hard work. . . . ."

After winning the British Open in 1926, Jones left real estate and made plans to enter Emory University School of Law in the fall. At the end of the fall term in 1927, halfway through the three-year program, Jones took the bar exam and passed. Prior to World War II, lawyers needed only to pass the bar, so Jones left Emory and was admitted to the bar on May 8, 1929. The next day he won his first federal case. Jones and his growing family lived for three years with his parents in a large home on Lullwater Road, near Mary's parents' home in the Druid Hills neighborhood of Atlanta. Their first child, Clara Malone, was born on April 18, 1925. A year later, on November 30, 1926, Bob Jones III was born. In November 1927, the Atlanta Athletic Club raised $50,000 as a gift to buy the Jones family a house, but Jones turned down the offer to avoid compromising his amateur status. In February 1928, the Jones family moved to 3501 Northside Drive. Mary Ellen, their third child, was born on January 19, 1931. The Jones family lived on Northside until 1939, and then moved to a house called Whitehall at 3425 Tuxedo Road that was designed for the Joneses by noted Atlanta architect Philip Shutze, famous for his 1928 design of the Swan House that is now part of the Atlanta History Center. The Jones family lived at Whitehall until Jones and Mary moved to an apartment at 2734 Peachtree Road in the summer of 1969.

Bobby Jones III at four weeks with his mother, Mary. Photo courtesy of the Jones family.

Despite his keen sense of humor and propensity for profanity, shown only to his closest friends, Jones was a formal man who would not allow his children to dine with their parents until they were eight and had learned appropriate table manners. Ivan Allen Jr., a former mayor of Atlanta and close friend of the Jones family, remembers, "Bob always stayed close to and spent a lot of time with his three children. There were many trips to the beach, and the movies, and the circus. In addition to attending PTA meetings, he was always available to help with homework."

Jones in front of his home on Northside Drive. Photo courtesy of Special Collections, Robert W. Woodruff Library, Emory University.

"He was a very gentle person. Whenever we kids had tantrums, he would always come and talk to us very gently, and that was much more effective than slapping us and anything like that. That's the main thing I can say about him, that he was a very gentle and wise person."

—CLARA BLACK

Charles Price once described him this way: "Jones read a lot of deep books, patronized the opera, and for a hobby, solved complex algebraic theorems the way other people did crossword puzzles. Still, there was nothing priggish or calculating about his behavior. He smoked to excess on the course, drank corn whiskey off it, and could listen to or tell an off-color story in the locker room. He was spontaneous, affectionate, and loyal to his friends." Jones learned his love of opera and classical music from his mother, Clara, who was a patron of the arts. He was also an avid quail hunter, often traveling to south Georgia to Robert Woodruff's Ichauway plantation. Jones fished regularly with Charlie Elliott, a writer for *Outdoor Life*, who served as the inspiration for Ed Dodd's comic strip, *Mark Trail*. Jones was a Georgia Tech football fan, and, with some lessons, eventually became an accomplished bridge player.

Jones, shown with two of his dogs, was an avid hunter. Photo courtesy of the USGA.

After passing the bar, Jones joined his father's law firm, Jones, Evins, Moore, and Powers (now Alston + Bird LLP), where he remained until his death in 1971, though he did not draw a salary because he spent so much time on outside projects. His office was modestly furnished, with few reminders of his golfing fame. One exception was a framed lithograph that included the final lines of "Alumnus Football," Rice's famous poem: "For when the One Great Scorer comes to mark against your name, / He writes—not that you won or lost—but how you played the game." After Jones determined that he was not suited for trial work, he focused on civil and contract law. In 1929, he

Jones at his desk in 1959. Photo courtesy of Special Collections, Robert W. Woodruff Library, Emory University.

became part-owner of the minor league baseball team, the Atlanta Crackers. Jones also supplemented his income with the *How I Play Golf* series that he made with Warner Brothers. The first group of 12 films netted more than $100,000, plus a percentage of the gross. For a second series of six films, titled *How to Break 90* and filmed in 1933, Jones was paid $60,000. Author Richard Miller estimates that the whole project eventually earned Jones about a quarter of a million dollars.

Jones also had an opportunity to use his mechanical engineering degree in partnership with A. G. Spalding and Brothers. In 1931, he signed on to help them design the first matched set of clubs, which were stamped "Robt. T. Jones, Jr.," and were available for purchase in 1932. On the market until 1973, it is estimated that Spalding sold more than 2 million sets of clubs in 15 different models. In 1932, Jones purchased a percentage of its stock and became a member of the board of directors. In 1936, he was asked by President Franklin D. Roosevelt to serve as an advisor to the Works Progress Administration (WPA), which worked to refurbish more than 600 municipal golf courses. Jones also served on the USGA Executive Committee from 1928 to 1930, and was a longtime member of the museum committee. In 1948, the year he played his last round of golf, Jones was named honorary chairman of the USGA's Amateur Public Links Championship.

When the United States entered World War II, Jones volunteered for the service and was inducted as a captain on June 5, 1942, into the U.S. Army. Since 1931, Jones had been a member of the U.S. Army Organized Reserve, but had not yet served. Jones worked for a short time in Jacksonville, Florida, as an aircraft warning service officer.

Bobby Jones' father remained his most enthusiastic supporter throughout his career. Photo courtesy of the USGA.

In the summer of 1943, he joined the Eighty-fourth Fighter Wing of the Ninth Tactical Air Command and moved to Harrisburg, Pennsylvania, for two months of additional training as a teletype operator and prisoner interrogator. Jones served as an intelligence officer in England and landed in Normandy on June 7, 1944, the day after D-Day. In sum, Jones spent about two months on the front lines and was promoted to the rank of lieutenant colonel. He was discharged and returned to Atlanta on August 25, 1944, when he learned that his father was ill.

During the war, Jones' parents moved in with Mary to help take care of the children.

Upon his return from Europe, Jones resumed his law practice, his work with Coca-Cola, and his position as a vice president of Spalding. In 1939 Jones purchased a franchise from the Coca-Cola Company to bottle and distribute the soft drink in New England. He later was a major stockholder in plants in Wisconsin and Glasgow, Scotland. His most profitable venture, though, was in 1945, when he invested money with 30 other businessmen, including

Jones fishing with football player Trig Hewett. Photo courtesy of the USGA.

Clifford Roberts, in Coca-Cola bottling plants in Uruguay, Argentina, and Chile. In 1952, Jones made his single foray into national politics, supporting Dwight D. Eisenhower for president. Three years later, Jones was asked to join the President's Conference on the Fitness of American Youth.

Of the Jones' three children, only their son, Bob, played golf with any vigor. Even though he was discouraged from taking up the game by his father, the young boy persisted and became a good amateur player. He won the Atlanta City Junior Championship in 1941 and several local club championships. He qualified for three U.S. Amateurs and, in 1959, lost in the first round, 7 and 6, to 18-year-old Jack Nicklaus. Bob Jones III attended Emory University and distinguished himself on its golf team for four years. For Jones' daughter Mary Ellen, however, golf was a different story. Longtime *Atlanta Journal-Constitution* columnist Furman Bisher recounted a story about Mary Ellen taking lessons from Stewart Maiden, who was hired as the golf professional at Peachtree Golf Club before it opened in 1948. Hoping to give his longtime friend and mentor some business, Jones sent Mary Ellen to Maiden for instruction. Making a sly reference to her father's 1960 book, she later joked, "Golf was *not* my game."

In the late forties, Jones began suffering from pain in his neck and shoulders. At the 1947 Masters, he noticed a stiffness that he had not experienced before. By July, he was unable to play golf. On October 30, 1948, Jones underwent surgery to remove a growth on his vertebrae at Emory University Hospital. On May 18, 1950, he had a second surgery at the Lahey Clinic in Boston to repair a damaged disc that seemed to be pressing on a nerve. Two years later, in the fall of 1952, Jones suffered a heart

Bobby and Mary Jones at Augusta National Golf Club in the forties.
Photo courtesy of the Jones family.

Bobby Jones III, pictured here with his father, was an accomplished amateur golfer. Photo courtesy of the Jones family.

attack. On June 13, 1956, he visited with Dr. H. Houston Merritt, the dean of the College of Physicians and Surgeons at the Columbia-Presbyterian Medical Center in New York and was diagnosed with syringomyelia. Over the years, his condition worsened, and he was forced to use one cane, then two canes, a leg brace, and eventually a wheelchair. He attended his last Masters in 1967. From April to December 1971, Jones was confined to his bed. On December 4, his abdominal aorta ruptured. Six days later, he converted to Catholicism, saying afterward to Monsignor McDonaugh of Atlanta's Cathedral of Christ the King, "You know, if I'd know how happy this has made Mary, I would have done it years ago." At 6:33 on the evening of December 18, 1971, Jones died quietly in his sleep at home from an aneurysm in his chest.

Jones lost so many of the people who were important to him before he passed away in 1971. His closest friend, O. B. Keeler, died October 15, 1950. Fellow Atlanta Athletic Club member Perry Adair died in 1953, followed the next year by Grantland Rice. In July 1956, his father, Colonel Bob Jones, died, and the law firm was incorporated into Bird and Howell. Jones assumed his father's legal work for the Jones Mercantile Company and Canton Textile Mills. In January 1961, Jones also lost his mother, Clara.

His wife, Mary, was diagnosed with cancer of the larynx in 1961, but was treated with radiation. She lived until May 23, 1975, after being rushed to the hospital with a bleeding peptic ulcer. All three of Jones' children survived him. Throughout his life, Bob Jones III was a nationally ranked amateur golfer and president of the Pittsfield Country Club in Massachusetts. In his professional life, he managed Coca-Cola bottling and distribution in western Massachusetts and

Bobby Jones III and Frances Massey on their wedding day. Photo courtesy of the Jones family.

Jones' children: (from left): Clara, Robert, and Mary Ellen.
Photo courtesy of the Jones family.

Vermont, and then made a career change in his forties to go into banking. Sadly, he died not long after on December 20, 1973, of a heart attack. As his daughter, Mary "Mimi" Frances Jones Hedwig, remembered, "The demands of caring for his ailing father and my chronically ill mother took their toll on his health. It was a great tragedy. He was an exacting father, but a loving one and the person who passed along to me the love of poetry and Shakespeare and the belief in the importance of living honorably that my grandfather had given to him." Mary Ellen Hood died of cancer on October 13, 1977. Clara, the last of Jones' children, died on February 10, 1994, also of cancer.

Each of Jones' children had children of their own. Clara and her husband, William Black, had three children: Merry E. Black, William Black Jr., and Clare Black McSwain. Robert Tyre III and his wife, Frances Massey, also had three children: Adele Walker Westbrook, Robert Tyre Jones IV, and Mimi Frances Jones Hedwig. Mary Ellen and her husband, Carl Hood, had one child, Anne Suttles Hood Laird. As time has passed, the family has grown to include great grandchildren. William Black and his wife, Patricia, have three children: William (Stewart), Robert, and Patricia (Tricia). Anne and her husband, Cody Laird, have four children: Cody Jr., Kate, Malone, and Madeline (Maddie). Robert Tyre Jones IV and his wife, Mary Delores (Mimi), have a daughter, Melanie. Adele has two children, Robert and Elizabeth. Mimi and her husband, Douglas Frederick Hedwig, have one son, Marcus.

The family continues to play an active role in preserving the Jones legacy. They have chosen a diverse range of professions, but they all have inherited the generosity of spirit that made their grandfather both famous and beloved.

Bub

by Merry E. Black

One of my first memories of my grandfather involved his canes. I could tell that they were important and necessary items, especially to get him to and from the office, which is the only place he went on any regular basis. He had to be helped out of the car by his driver, and slowly he would shuffle, one step at a time, into the house, across the large entry, down a few steps, and across the living room to a little wooden door hidden in a back corner of the house. There he would get inside a small elevator, large enough for only one person. Up he would ascend, out of sight. I would run back through the living room and fly up the stairs to be there just as he emerged into the bedroom. Slowly and painstakingly he would find his way to a small room off the back, which was referred to as the "sanctum." Finally, home from the office, he could rest in the chair. Now there was time for a cigarette and a drink. Now everyone can sit and talk. After the canes came the braces—big, ugly metal things with shoes attached. I found them interestingly awkward and tried to put them on and walk as he did. I am sure everyone found my fascination a little disturbing, but I was left alone to discover why he needed such devices. On Sundays our family often visited my grandparents' home. My grand-

Jones in his library at his house on Tuxedo Road.
Photo courtesy of the Atlanta History Center.

father would occasionally instill upon us words of wisdom; he was not the kind of man who would dote, cuddle, or spoil. He was much like an oracle, sitting in his chair. In the afternoons, a golf tournament would come on the television and everything would stop for three hours. I did not understand the appeal, but he was totally absorbed. Several years later, a wheelchair replaced the braces. The cigarettes were now lined up in a neat row on a table in front of his chair, each with a holder to help his crippled hands grip them better. Occasionally, we were told that Bub wasn't feeling well and he was to be left alone. As his illness progressed, you could see the pain in his face and you could hear a muffled groan, but I never heard a selfish complaint.

~5~
The Freedom
of the City

IN 1958, BOBBY JONES HAD NOT played a full round of golf for a decade. A family man, he was still active in his law practice and enjoyed fishing and watching Georgia Tech football with his children. He continued to write on golf, serve as the host for The Masters in April, and spend time with his friends at the Atlanta Athletic and Peachtree Golf clubs. Suffering from the effects of syringomyelia, he was unable to stand or walk without assistance. It did not, however, prevent him from being named the nonplaying captain of the American team of the first World Amateur Team Championship, which featured teams from 29 countries. The competition was to be a 72-hole stroke-play event. Because of Jones' limited mobility, the organizers of the event obtained a motorized golf cart that would allow him to follow the American team around the course. He was delighted to return to St. Andrews because he "felt that this might be my last opportunity to revisit the city and golf course that I love so well." On October 13, the Americans lost by two strokes to the Australian team, 222–224, in an 18-hole playoff. Jones later complimented the opponents, saying, "The young men from Australia were a fine group and deserved the honor. Everybody got along fine." But the championship was simply a footnote to what had happened the week before.

St. Andrews and Scotland meant a great deal to Jones. Herbert Warren Wind once remarked on "this quite unique love affair between an athlete and a town." But Jones' relationship to St. Andrews had not begun well. After his first encounter with the Old Course, he later confessed that he "considered St. Andrews among the very worst courses I have ever seen, and I am afraid I was even disrespectful of its difficulty." That initial disrespect turned into a disqualification for Jones in 1921 at the age of 19. John Companiotte, in an article for the 2002 March/April issue of *Golf Journal*, recounts a less-publicized incident in the same championship. Jones missed a three-foot putt on the 16th hole, tossed his putter on the ground, and began to leave the green. Jock Hutchison, a noted professional and the eventual victor in the Open, caught up with Jones and severely reprimanded him for his behavior. When Jones triumphantly returned to St. Andrews six years later, in 1927, to win the British Open, he recalled Hutchison's lecture as a turning point in his career. After Jones' retirement, Hutchison was regularly invited to play in The Masters and became the honorary starter in 1963 with Fred McLeod.

Jones, captain of the U.S. team competing for the Eisenhower Trophy, on October 6, 1958. Photo courtesy of the Associated Press.

In 1926, the year before his win at his first major championship at St. Andrews, Jones played the Old Course again for the Walker Cup matches. Then, he seemed to have come to terms with the nuances of links golf. In 1960, Jones wrote of the Old Course, "I think it was not long before I began to see her as a wise old lady, whimsically tolerant of my impatience, but all the while ready to reveal to me the secrets of her complex being, if I would only take the trouble to study and to learn." The Walker Cup in 1926 became Jones' classroom. For the first-day foursomes, Jones and his fellow club member from Atlanta, Watts Gunn, defeated Cyril Tolley and Andrew Jamieson Jr., 4 and 3. The next day, in the singles match, Jones bested Tolley, 12 and 11. After that victory,

The city of St. Andrews in the twenties. Photo courtesy of the University of St. Andrews.

Jones, Watts Gunn, Cyril Tolley, and Andrew Jamieson Jr. at the 1926 Walker Cup in St. Andrews. Photo courtesy of the USGA.

Jones being carried above the crowd after winning the 1927 British Open. Photo courtesy of Special Collections, Robert W. Woodruff Library, Emory University.

Jones called the Old Course "the finest course I have ever played." When Jones returned to St. Andrews in 1927, he was the defending British Open champion, having won the previous year at Royal Lytham and St. Anne's Golf Club. He opened in 1927 with a 68 and kept the lead throughout the championship, winning by six strokes. At the presentation, he said, "Nothing would make me happier than to take home your trophy. But I cannot. It was played here for 30 years before I was born. Please honor me by allowing it to be kept here at the Royal and Ancient

"The quality of sportsmanship is the quality I would most want to be praised for."

—BOBBY JONES

A bird's-eye view of St. Andrews during the 1930 British Amateur.
Photo courtesy of Special Collections, Robert W. Woodruff Library, Emory University.

Golf Club where it belongs." The Scots agreed to allow the R&A, of which Jones was an honorary member, to keep the trophy, and Jones won the hearts and minds of the people in the town forever.

Three years later, in 1930, St. Andrews became the site of what Jones called "the most important achievement of my life." In his 14 years of competitive play, Jones had never won the British Amateur, and it was the first leg of what came to be known as the Grand Slam in 1930. Winning it would propel him toward his goal. His victory over Tolley prompted Jones to declare at the trophy ceremony, "I must say how happy I am to have won this cup. I've never worked harder or suffered more than in trying to get it." Several months after the event, Jones received a wooden box containing a miniature of the British Amateur trophy with a note that read, "To Robert Tyre Jones, Jr., a golfer matchless in skill and chivalrous in spirit, from some fellow members of the Royal and Ancient Golf Club."

Jones' retirement in 1930 did not dampen the Scots' enthusiasm for their "Bonnie Bobby." In 1936, the mutual adoration of the city and Jones was evident. On the boat across the Atlantic on the way to Berlin in 1936 to watch

Spectators rushing along the Old Course to see Jones capture the British Amateur. Photo courtesy of Special Collections, Robert W. Woodruff Library, Emory University.

the Olympic Games with Grantland and Kate Rice, Jones met up with Robert and Nell Woodruff, who were traveling to Gleneagles Golf Course in Scotland. The Joneses joined them, and the party drove to St. Andrews for lunch and an afternoon round. When word spread throughout the town that Jones was back, more than two thousand locals rushed to the course to see him play again. Those who remained in town found signs that read "Our Bobby Is Back" in closed shop windows. Woodruff reported on the day: "Bob just went out at St. Andrews for a practice

Bobby Jones at the Royal and Ancient Golf Club of St. Andrews
by Peter Lewis

On June 4, 1926, the day after the Walker Cup match had finished at St. Andrews, Norman Boase, the chairman of the Royal and Ancient Golf Club's Championship Committee, proposed four men for membership to the club. They were William Fownes, president of the USGA, Charles Pfeil, vice president of the USGA, Robert Gardner, the American Walker Cup captain, and Bobby Jones. All four were seconded by Robert Harris, the 1925 Amateur champion, and duly elected as members on August 4, 1926.

That date marked the beginning of a very special relationship between Jones, the Royal and Ancient Golf Club, and the town of St. Andrews. In early 1934 Jones donated the driver he had used "in many championships" to the club, which was gratefully accepted and is now on display in the British Golf Museum. Twenty years later, in 1954, Jones loaned the club a copy of the Thomas E. Stephens portrait of Francis Ouimet, who became the first American captain of the club in 1951.

What made the copy special was that it had been painted by the president of the United States, Dwight Eisenhower, who had been made an honorary member of the R&A in 1945. The loan of the painting was rapidly converted into a gift in early 1956.

At the general committee meeting on March 9, 1956, it was agreed to invite Jones to become an honorary member of the club. Jones accepted the invitation. Normally honorary members did not have to pay the annual subscription, but Jones expressed a typically generous desire to continue to pay it. After discussions with Clifford Roberts, the club decided to commission a portrait of Bobby Jones in his prime to be executed from photographs, and London based artist Arthur Mills was commissioned. The portrait was finished by March 18, 1966, and the club was pleased with it. Photographs of the portrait were sent to Roberts and Jones as had been previously agreed and both wrote back expressing their pleasure in it.

"He was the only celebrity I ever knew who was prepared to accept as gracefully as possible every penalty there is to be paid for fame and publicity in the United States. . . . He was a gentleman and there was laughter in his heart and on his lips, and he loved his friends."

—PAUL GALLICO

round. There wasn't any announcement of it. But, before he had gone two holes, the gallery was large and growing every minute. And every blessed Scot in it was beaming of face and talking fondly about him." Jones was paired with Willie Auchterlonie, the club professional at the R&A, and Gordon Lockhart from Gleneagles. Lockhart withdrew after a few holes, but Auchterlonie played the entire round. Jones shot a 32 on the front nine and a 40 on the back, and later remarked, "I have ever been thankful that for at least part of what was to be my last golfing at St. Andrews I was permitted to play so well." The 8th hole was the most memorable for Jones. With a 4 iron, he drove within nine feet of the hole. As he stepped off the tee, Jones' caddie muttered, "My, but you're a wonder, Sir." After the round, Jones stayed in the clubhouse for a short while, signing autographs. In the half century since

The Silver Casket and Burgess Ticket

The silver casket and burgess ticket awarded to Bobby Jones are the centerpieces of the Atlanta History Center's exhibition, Down the Fairway with Bobby Jones. Hamilton and Inches of Edinburgh, Scotland, made the casket, which includes the coat of arms of St. Andrews on the lid. An inscription on the side reads:

Presented by the Royal Burgh of St. Andrews to Robert Tyre Jones, jun., with the Freedom of the City. 9th October 1958. R. Leonard, Provost.

The burgess ticket, a parchment scroll, was designed by Waddie and Company of Edinburgh, and it reads:

At St. Andrews, the ninth day of October, nineteen hundred and fifty-eight, which day Robert Tyre Jones, junior, of Atlanta, Georgia was by the Provost, Magistrates and Councillors of the Royal Burgh of St. Andrews presented with the freedom of the city and admitted as an Honorary Burgess thereof, in recognition of his incomparable skill in the game of golf, the universal esteem in which he is held by golfers throughout the world, and the tribute which his fellow-countrymen have paid to St. Andrews by inaugurating here the first World Amateur Golf Team Championship. In witness whereof the said Provost, Magistrates and Councillors have authorized Robert Leonard, Provost, and Neil Charles Henry Mackenzie, Town-Clerk, to subscribe these presents on their behalf, and to affix the city's seal therto. Signed Robert Leonard, Provost. N.C.H. Mackenzie, Town Clerk.

Roger Wethered congratulating Jones on his victory in the British Amateur on May 31, 1930. Photo courtesy of Special Collections, Robert W. Woodruff Library, Emory University.

My Grandfather's House
by Merry E. Black

When I visited my grandparents' house, I would ramble about the rooms to entertain myself while my parents and grandparents talked about the day's news or an upcoming bridge game. There were interesting rooms filled with books, antiques, and memories. I distinctly remember the library, the only room that harbored any golf memorabilia. There was a globe with little flags on it that marked the Grand Slam tournaments. There was the large painting of him above a desk. And there were books, so many books about literature, opera, history, and war. They were boring titles to a child. There was also a small box that contained some medals from amateur competitions, nothing of note to me at that age. And then there was the little silver box that we called the "the casket." Inside was a scroll that was neatly rolled up and tied, and somehow we all knew that it was special because it was from St. Andrews. I read it and found it exquisitely beautiful, but it did not mean much to me until later in life. I do, however, know that it meant the world to him.

Provost Robert Leonard (right) presenting the Freedom of the City to Bobby Jones. Photo courtesy of the Associated Press.

Jones last set foot in St. Andrews, the adoration has not abated. Companiotte quotes John Philp, a St. Andrews native and employee of Links Golf St. Andrews, as saying, "Jones' name enters conversations about the game so easily that you expect to see him strolling down one of the side streets."

Twenty-two years after his 1936 visit, Jones returned to the city of St. Andrews that he so loved for the last time.

When his plans became public, Neil Charles Henry Mackenzie, the town clerk of St. Andrews, cabled Jones on September 9, to ask if he would accept the Freedom of the City of the Royal Burgh of St. Andrews, an honor that had, until then, been reserved for statesmen, men of letters, and scientists. Assuming it would be the equivalent of the key to the city that was bestowed upon him by various municipalities, he kindly accepted. Jones was warmly greeted by

The Freedom of the City ceremony was held in Younger Hall in St. Andrews. Photo courtesy of the Jones family.

the Scots, including Johnnie Law and Jack McIntyre, his former caddies. The day after his arrival, on October 4, he met in the afternoon with Robert Leonard, the provost of St. Andrews, the equivalent of the city's mayor, and learned that the only other American ever to receive the honor was Benjamin Franklin—199 years earlier. Jones began to "get an inkling of what was meant by Freedom of the City." His

of the audience and became determined to "stuff some notes into my pocket, just in case of dire emergency."

On October 9, 1958, on a cool Thursday evening at Younger Graduation Hall on the campus of the University of St. Andrews, nearly seventeen hundred people representing 30 countries gathered for the ceremony. The audience was comprised of the 116 players of the world cup team and the

"I had no earthly idea what was meant by the Freedom of the City. I assumed it was something like the presentation in this country of the key to the city, which is largely an excuse to have the visitor's, and incidentally, the mayor's, picture printed in the afternoon newspaper. But whatever the nature of the ceremony was to be, I was happy indeed to accept any gesture of hospitality which might be extended to me by St. Andrews."

—BOBBY JONES

new awareness of the significance of the honor prompted him to confess that "at this point the matter was assuming alarming proportions." After several other meetings and rehearsals over the next several days, the provost presented Jones with a copy of his speech, and the town clerk requested a copy of what Jones was going to say. Struggling to come up with the words, Jones explained, "I had not been able to produce anything that I felt would be suitable, my experience having always been that nothing appropriate can be written without the help of having the feel of the actual situation." Later, Jones confessed that he was worried that he would "draw a complete blank" in front

delegates from various countries. Five hundred tickets were sold in less than two hours to the townspeople of St. Andrews, who had gathered to see Jones receive the honor. Hundreds of others were gathered outside the hall and on the streets, hoping to glimpse their hero. Since his retirement from competitive golf, Jones had been inducted into numerous halls of fame and been given a variety of honors that recognized his skill as an athlete and his contributions as a citizen of the world. But none matched the Freedom of the City.

At 8:00 in the evening, Provost Leonard, dressed in a crimson robe with an ermine collar and chain signifying his office around his neck, led the procession that included

Jones, local town dignitaries, the copresidents of the World Golf Association, Jones' wife, and their two younger children. (Their eldest daughter, Clara, had to remain in Atlanta to care for her two small children and could not make the trip.) Jones and Leonard were seated in high-backed chairs at a table on either sides of the lectern where the presentation would take place. Members of the town council, the principal of the University of St. Andrews, Sir George Cunningham, and other members of the Royal and Ancient Club and Joint Links Committee were also seated on the platform.

The ceremony started simply with a prayer, delivered by Reverend Dr. Rankin. Mackenzie, the town clerk, dressed formally in a white wig, read the burgess ticket. In addition to the right to chase rabbits in the city limits of St. Andrews, the honor bestowed upon Jones the privilege "to cart shells, to take divots, and to dry one's own washing upon the first and last fairways of the Old Course." Provost Leonard spoke first, simply and without hyperbole. He then rolled the small scroll, which the town clerk had read, placed it in a silver box called a casket, and presented it to Jones. Though nearly crippled, Jones rose of his own accord, accepted the casket, placed it on the table in front of him, and returned to his seat to sign the Burgess' Roll, just under the name of Stanley Baldwin, the former British prime minister who had been given the honor 28 years prior. The provost turned to Jones, smiled, and said, "Now, Bob, the ordeal is yours." It was Jones' turn at the podium.

Journalists Henry Longhurst and Herbert Warren Wind were present at the ceremony, and Longhurst later declared that it "was one of the most moving occasions in the memory of those of us who were lucky enough to be there." Wind recalled later:

> Bobby spoke for about 10 minutes, beautifully and movingly. He left the stage and got into his electric golf cart. As he directed it down the aisle to leave, the whole hall spontaneously burst into the old Scottish song "Will Ye No' Come Back Again?" So honestly heartfelt was this reunion for Bobby Jones and the people of St. Andrews (and for everyone) that it was 10 minutes before many who attended were able to speak again in a tranquil voice.

Jones would never return to Europe again, and within a few years, he would be confined to his home.

In *Golf Is My Game*, Jones recalled the day in his chapter titled, "St. Andrews: A Short Love Story." He said of the ceremony:

> I am not the least bit ashamed to admit that I had been deeply moved by the ceremony—as much as by the awareness of the depth and sincerity of my affection for these people as by their expressions to me. It is a wonderful experience to go about a town where people wave at you from doorways and windows, where strangers smile and greet you by name, often your first name, and where a simple and direct courtesy is the outstanding characteristic.

The dedication of the 10th hole on the Old Course after Jones' death. Photo courtesy of the Atlanta Athletic Club.

Presentation Remarks of Robert Leonard, Provost
St. Andrews, Scotland

Ladies and gentlemen, we are met here today to confer the Freedom of the City and Royal Burgh of St. Andrews on Mr. Robert Tyre Jones, Junior of Atlanta, Georgia.

Among its many other claims to renown St. Andrews has for long been recognized as the metropolis of the golfing world—and its selection for the first international competition for the Eisenhower Trophy at the generous request of its American originators is further confirmation of this fact. Mr. Jones is recognized as the most distinguished golfer of this age—one might say of all time. Thus it is appropriate that just such a place and just such a personality should be linked together at just such a time as this.

But the conferring of the freedom of a city, although it may have a certain formal symbolism of this kind, can never be a merely formal matter—and it can rarely have been less so on this occasion. As representatives of the community of St. Andrews we wish to honor Mr. Jones because we feel drawn to him by ties of affection and personal regard of a particularly cordial nature, and because we know that he himself has declared his own enduring affection for this place and for its people.

Like many cordial and enduring partnerships, it was not, I think, a case of love at first sight. Probably few St. Andreans paid much attention to the visit of a relatively unknown young American golfer for the British Open Championship of 1921, and I believe that for his part the first impression that Mr. Jones formed of the Old Course was something less than favorable. And there—with any other person and any other place— the matter might well have rested. But back he came in 1927 to master the intricacies of golf at St. Andrews as they had never been mastered before, even by our own giants of the nineteenth century, and to win his way not only to the Open Championship but to the hearts of St. Andrews people from that day to this.

Even now, more than thirty years later, it is possible to recapture the thrill of that occasion in Mr. Bernard Darwin's incomparable prose.

As he says—and remember that he is writing of the days before crowd control, when great multitudes surged over the Old Course in pursuit of their favorites—"Many vivid pictures remain in my mind's eye from this day, but there is one in particular. Bobby lay just short of the home green in the hollow called the Valley of Sin. He ran his long putt up dead and the crowd stormed up the slope and waited breathless for a moment on the crest. He popped his ball in, and the next instant there was to be seen no green and no Bobby—nothing but a black and seething mass, from which there ultimately emerged the victor borne on enthusiastic shoulders and holding his famous putter 'Calamity Jane' over his head in a frantic effort to preserve it."

Three years later, in 1930, when he won both the Open and the Amateur Championships of Britain and America alike—a feat never accomplished before or since—it was here that Mr. Jones attained what he himself probably regarded as the most perilous and desirable among these four contests for an American—the British Amateur Championship—a win that was acclaimed in St. Andrews almost as the triumph of a favorite son.

Nothing could ever surpass the achievement of that memorable year—the climax of seven years scarcely less memorable, in every one of which he had won a major award. Let me detail them: the American Open in 1923, and the Amateur in 1924 and 1925, the American and the British Open in 1926, the American Amateur and the British Open in 1927, the American Amateur again in 1928, and the Open again in 1929; finally, all four in 1930.

And so, at the height of his attainments, and still at the height of his powers, Mr. Jones retired from major competitive events—to reign forever after in our hearts, as Mr. Darwin suggests, as the Champion of Champions to the end of his days.

And so we feel that when we welcome back Mr. Jones to St. Andrews we welcome an old and dearly loved friend—as we welcomed him on his last visit in 1936 when he played round the Old Course attended, one might well imagine, by practically the entire population of the town.

We welcome him for his own sake; we welcome him also as an ambassador in the cause of international understanding and goodwill which the competition of this week is designed to promote. We welcome him, moreover, not only as a distinguished golfer, but as a man of outstanding character, courage, and accomplishment, well worthy to adorn the roll of our honorary burgesses. And that an American should once again be entered in that roll may well be thought timely, for it is just one year short of two hundred years ago, in October 1759, that our predecessors welcomed Dr. Benjamin Franklin of Philadelphia and accorded him the privileges of a burgess and guild brother of the City of St. Andrews.

What these privileges now are, in any tangible sense, even the Town Clerk hesitates to suggest—though Mr. Jones may be interested to know that any that are ever mentioned relate specifically to the Links—to cart shells, to take divots, and to dry one's washing upon the first and last fairways of the Old Course.

These are homely terms—and perhaps in an American as well as a British sense—but they may help us to convey to our new honorary burgess just what we mean by this freedom ceremony—that he is free to feel at home in St. Andrews as truly as in his own first home town of Atlanta, one of our own number officially now as he has been so long unofficially.

Photo courtesy of the Jones family.

Acceptance Remarks of Bobby Jones
St. Andrews, Scotland

The provost has given me permission to tell you that, lacking a middle initial of his own, he will, in future, be known as Robert T. Leonard. I consider that the greatest triumph I have ever won in Scotland.

People of St. Andrews, I know that you are doing me a very high honor and I want you to know that I am very grateful for it. I appreciate the fact that my good friend, the provost, has glossed over my first encounter with the Old Course, but I would like you to know that I did not say a lot of things that were put out I had said. But I could not play the course, and I did not think any-one else could. I ask you to remember, of course, that at the time I had attained the ripe old age of 19 years, and I did not know much about golf.

Actually, that first time, we got along pretty good, the Old Course and me, for two rounds. I scored 151—of course there was no wind. My boys here this week will admit that ain't bad.

But I started off in the third round and the wind was blowing right in my face. That day it was really blowing! I reached the turn in 43, and when I was play-ing the 7th, 8th, and 9th, I thought, "Well, that's fine, I'll be blowing home with the wind." Well, as I stood on the 10th tee it turned right round and it blew home all the way against me. I got a 6 at the 10th, and then, at the 11th, I put my shot into Hill Bunker, not Strath, as they said. They also say that when I got out of that bunker I hit my ball into the Eden. That's not so, for I never did get the ball out of Hill Bunker.

I came back to the Old Course in 1926 to practice for the Walker Cup, but before that I had done a lot of thinking and talking to a lot of transplanted Scots who knew St. Andrews. I set about studying it and I pretty soon found out that local knowledge is a real important thing if you want to play that golf course. You have to study it, and the more you study the more you learn; the more you learn the more you study it. I have to say this of the Old Course, that after my chastisement she seemed to be satisfied for she never let me lose another contest. When I say that, I mean what she did to the other fellow.

But the memories of St. Andrews that really mean most to me—I am afraid to talk about them because I get a little too emotional—are not entirely to do with championships. After all, you know if you enter a tour-nament and don't cheat, and happen to make the lower score, they have to give you the cup.

But you people of St. Andrews have a sensitivity and an ability to extend cordiality in an ingenious way. When I won the Amateur in 1930 and got back home, I received, through the post, a perfect miniature of the Amateur Championship Trophy. It was an exquisite thing, perfect in every detail, down to the names inscribed on it. There was an inscription on it which, at this moment, I could not trust myself to repeat. That miniature came to me with the simple message that it was from fellow members of the R&A. It has remained my prized possession.

Then I have another great memory. In 1936 I set out with my wife to go to the Olympic Games in Berlin. Of course, I took my clubs along with me because in those days they were very necessary impedimenta. We met some friends and planned to spend two days at Gleneagles. Well, we played two rounds there. Then I told my friends I could not be this close to St. Andrews without making a pilgrimage to it. We got here before noon and had lunch. I had been playing perfectly dread-ful golf, too, I can tell you. Anyhow, we finished lunch and walked over to the first tee—and there were waiting about two thousand people.

I said to myself, "This is an awful thing to do to my friends if they have come to see me golf with the dreadful stuff I am playing." Anyway, Willie Auchterlonie and Gordon Lockhart started off with me, but Gordon stopped after two holes. By that time the crowd was about four thousand. Such a spontaneous show of warmth and affection I have never known in my life. It was such a splendid welcome you people gave me that I played the best golf I had played for four years, and certainly never since. I had a 3 at the 2nd—I'm not bragging. Then I got to the 6th—in those days we were playing the old tee and I still think it's the better tee. I say so for this reason, that the second shot you have to play then is the old St. Andrews run-up shot. I said to myself, "Look, Jones, these people are all expecting you to play that run-up, so don't funk it."

I can tell you it was with considerable misgivings that I played the shot, but that ball ran up and on the green and it finished six feet from the flag. I holed it for a 3. That, and my score, were just nothing but the inspiration of playing at St. Andrews. I went out in 32 and had a 2 at the 8th. I was so happy and in a transport almost that when I reached the 11th I went over Strath going for the green and landed in a bunker that no longer exists. It was about 15 feet from the hole and I went out looking for that bunker the other day and the greenkeeper told me it had never been there. I said to him, "You can't tell me that, because I played two shots in it in 1936."

That was a great day for me—and now I have this. I could take out of my life everything except my experiences at St. Andrews and I would still have had a rich and full life.

You know that two very important words in the English language that are much abused, illused, or misused—*friend* and *friendship*. When I say to a person, "I am your friend," I've said about the ultimate. When I say, "You are my friend," I may be assuming too much. Maybe that's a responsibility that you do not want to accept. But when I've said as much about you, and you've done so much for me, I'd think that when I say or I use the word *friend*, that you are my friend and I'm your friend. When I say you're my friend under these circumstances, I'm at the same time affirming my affection and regard for you and expressing my complete faith in you and my trust in the sincerity of your friendship, so therefore I say to you, greetings my friends of St. Andrews.

Bob, I hope I have not been too sentimental on this theme of friendship, but it is one that is so important at this time. It is another element of the sensitivity that you people have—a wonderful, warm relationship. Friendship should be the great note of this world golf meeting, because not only people, but nations need friends. Let us hope that this meeting will sow seeds which will germinate and grow into important friendships between nations later on.

I just want to say to you that this is the finest thing that has ever happened to me. Whereas that little cup was first in my heart, now this will be in my heart, and then the memory of 1936, so I guess you could say in my house St. Andrews will take win, place, and show. I like to think about it this way, too, as I have several times, that now, to paraphrase your closing words, now I officially have the right to feel as much at home here as I have presumed to feel unofficially for a number of years. Thank you.

~6~

The Legacy of
Bobby Jones

"I was naturally drawn to the exploits of Bob Jones, and I remember thinking if I could fashion a golf career along the lines of his, that would be a dream come true."

—ARNOLD PALMER

IN AN ERA RIFE WITH SPORTS scandals, Bobby Jones remains a role model worthy of respect and emulation. Atlanta businessman John P. Imlay Jr., who has been instrumental in preserving the Jones legacy at the Atlanta History Center, says of Jones, "He lived a life worth living." In an article for *The New Yorker* celebrating the 50th anniversary of the Grand Slam, Herbert Warren Wind asked a question of Jones that is still relevant today: "How is it that he remains so alive for us and that what he did in 1930 continues to hold meaning for us and to give us pleasure?"

Jones lived his life in Atlanta, the heart of the South. With the exception of his time studying at Harvard and his short winter jaunts to Sarasota, Florida, while working in real estate in the twenties, his brief stints in Hollywood in the thirties, and his wartime service in the forties, he spent his whole life in Atlanta, never moving more than 10 miles from the house in which he was born. It is certainly an understatement to say that Atlanta is a different place in 2005 than it was in 1930, when Jones won the Grand Slam. He was, for some people, one of the most important people to come out of the South since the Civil War. The city was only a few decades removed from the Atlanta race riot of 1906. The year Jones defeated his father in the Atlanta Athletic Club Championship at East Lake was also the year of the Leo Frank lynching, which took place only 20 miles from downtown. While Atlanta today leads the nation's economic recovery, the South of Bobby Jones was only two generations beyond the devastation of the Civil War. Jones may well have been the best-loved Southerner since Robert E. Lee, but, unlike Lee, his legacy is not tainted with defeat. Instead, Jones came to represent the city on the cusp of prosperity.

There is no doubt that Jones, with his exemplary sportsmanship and intellect, stands above his fellow athletes of the twenties. Additionally, as a part of the newly developed cult of celebrity of the Jazz Age that included Babe Ruth, Henry Ford, and Rudolph Valentino, he was perceived as more human and more respectable than his famous counterparts. Comparing Jones to another hero of the twenties, Charles Lindbergh, may also help explain Jones' appeal. On the morning of May 20, 1927, "Lucky Lindy," left Long Island in his monoplane, the *Spirit of St. Louis*. Nearly 34 hours later, he landed outside Paris, captured the public's imagination, and ushered in the era of modern aviation. But Lindbergh's eventual support of Nazi Germany, like Ruth's womanizing and Ford's xenophobia, would forever taint his reputation. Jones, in contrast, never lost his luster. In fact, with each decade his legend seems to shine brighter.

Jones' commitment to amateurism also contributed to his reputation. H. J. Whigham, in his 1909 article, "American Sport from an English Point of View," published in *Outlook*, distinguished, with some arrogance, between sports: "Baseball, boxing, and many of our common sports trace their origin to common people who possessed no code of honor. On the other hand, golf and tennis, historically gentlemen's games, have come down to us

according to *Bobby Jones—Stroke of Genius* producer John Shepherd, fall into a trap of "telling the story of a good man getting gooder."

Jones' example is an antidote to the sporting world's troubled present. Sports have always been tainted by corruption, as evidenced by Ty Cobb's suspension from playing with the Detroit Tigers in 1912 for beating up a heckler and the more infamous Black Sox scandal of 1919. But problems in sports have become more common. Widespread doping scandals diminished the 2004 Summer Olympics in Greece; baseball players have been punished for altercations with fans, umpires, and other players; numerous athletes have faced rape charges; and Pete Rose's confessional memoir

"It is the story of an ancient game's greatest champion, an extraordinary human being of exceeding talents reaching far beyond incomparable sporting feats."

—AL LANEY, 1972

so interwoven with a high code of honor that we have been forced to accept the code along with the game." While Whigham's class bias explains his disdain for the origins of "common sport," he is correct in recognizing a code that pervades golf. None symbolized this ideal better than Jones, yet he was never considered an affluent, snobbish dandy, a common criticism leveled at amateur athletes in America. According to historian Stephen Lowe, Jones' life "was nearly a perfect reflection of the finest traditional values." This may explain why many fans of Jones,

about gambling deeply influenced the way modern audiences feel about sport. Jones' restraint, intellect, and modesty certainly would be worthy of emulation in today's world of professional sports, but he also stood heads above his contemporaries. Red Grange, Babe Ruth, and Ty Cobb were extraordinary athletes, but they were not extraordinary men. In many ways, Jones was.

Jones left the competition at the peak of his game, avoiding what A. E. Housman warns against in the fifth stanza of his famous poem, "To an Athlete Dying Young":

Now you will not swell the rout
of lads that wore their honours out,
Runners whom renown outran
And the name died before the man.

Unlike Housman's hero, Jones did not die young, but quietly became a private citizen. In contrast to Muhammad Ali or Michael Jordan, Jones never contemplated a comeback and was content to retire from competition at the age of 28 to focus on his family, his law practice and business ventures, and his city. His identity was not determined by golf. This was largely because of his class status; becoming a professional golfer was not a legitimate career choice for him.

Prior to World War II, tournament organizers made distinctions between amateur and professional golfers. In 1930, the U.S. Open program bestowed amateurs with the title "Mr.," but denied it to their professional competitors. This snobbery was largely because of the professional players' working-class backgrounds. Walter Hagen and Gene Sarazen, two of Jones' contemporaries, were the sons of a blacksmith and recent Italian immigrants, respectively. With a few notable exceptions, professionals were not widely respected by golf's governing bodies or country clubs until a decade after Jones' retirement. Comparing Jones to professional athletes of today is ultimately a futile exercise, but it does bring the amateur ideal into sharp relief, suggesting that there is no equivalent professional code of conduct that transcends sport. Longtime *Atlanta Journal-Constitution* columnist Furman Bisher explains, "Bobby Jones represented the true gentleman sportsman of his time. No punching the air with his fist, cap waving,

> *"The essence of the man might well have been that he embodied the spirit of golf more than anyone who ever played the game."*
>
> —*JACK NICKLAUS*

wide-mouthed shouts of self-acclamation, but a pleased smile after he sank his putt."

While O. B. Keeler is often remembered as the main architect of Jones' legacy, Grantland Rice, the most famous sportswriter of the twenties, played as significant a role in crafting Jones' image in an era that made athletes rival Greek gods. Rice once wrote, "When a sportswriter stops making heroes out of athletes, it's time to get out of the business." That sentiment is not widely shared by today's sportswriters, who are accustomed to widespread greed and corruption in sport, which helps explain why Jones was—and is—so revered. Rice's theory of sport meshed with Jones' ethic of amateurism. In *Colliers* in 1925, Rice wrote, "The main idea back of sport should be recreation in pursuit of health and pleasure: competitions that help to build up clean living, cool heads, stout hearts, and sound judgment under fire. Victory is, of course, the more pleasing destiny, but it isn't the entire destiny."

Newspaper audiences, reeling from World War I, embraced Rice's philosophy and looked to sport as a kind of return to the innocence of play. Rice explained in a June 1919 essay in *Country Life*, "With the return of peace it was only natural that there should be a great rush back to sport again. There was first of all an almost universal desire for recreation and play. There was also a great desire for the thrills of competition not quite so closely associated with death and devastation, where it was more man against man, rather than man against machine." But there was more to it. As Mark Inabinett explains in *Grantland Rice and His Heroes: The Sportswriter as Mythmaker in the 1920s*, "The first year after the war's end brought changes and uncertainty: the Treaty of Versailles, prohibition, women's suffrage, race riots, and red scares. Sociologists contend the combination created a need for visible symbols of stability." Sport, with its exuberant and optimistic spirit, seemed a logical choice. Herbert Hoover concurred, "Next to religion, the single greatest factor for good in the United States in recent years has been sport." Prior to the war, the American heroes were largely drawn from industry, arts and letters, and science. After the war, they were drawn from baseball diamonds, golf courses, and race tracks. Sportswriters obliged, shaping public opinion through colorful reporting that verged on mythmaking.

In 1936, writer Paul Gallico mused about his approach to writing about sport, "We sing of their muscles, their courage, their gameness, and their skill because it seems to amuse readers and sell papers, but we rarely consider them as people and strictly speaking leave their characters alone because that is dangerous ground." That was certainly true for Ty Cobb or Shoeless Joe Jackson, but not for Jones. This may be best illustrated by his courage in the face of adversity long after he left golf. From the age of 46 until his death in 1971, Jones struggled with the painful effects of syringomyelia, a degenerative spinal disease. Despite his

limited mobility, increasing pain, and dependency on assistance for even the most basic daily tasks, he never lost his humor, as Richard Miller explained in his book, *Triumphant Journey*: "His laughter refused to die—it was still young and spontaneous, always seeming to burst forth at just the right time to ease a guest at an awkward moment and chase away any feeling of pity one might have for him." Jones' demeanor helps explain why he drew so many fans outside of the world of sport. As Wind once observed, "Everybody adored him—not just dyed-in-the-wool golfers, but people who had never struck a golf ball or had the least desire to. They admired the ingrained modesty, the humor, the generosity of spirit that were evident in Jones' remarks and deportment. They liked the way he looked, this handsome, clean-cut young man, whose eyes gleamed with both a frank boyishness and a perceptiveness far beyond his years." One other explanation for the continued interest in Jones' life is the passage of time. As the generation of people who knew Jones slowly passes away, there is a particular urgency to chronicle his life. This same urgency encourages historians to interview what Tom Brokaw calls the Greatest Generation, those who served in World War II or survived the Holocaust.

Since his death, Jones has been the subject of numerous celebrations, programs, and scholarships. No other athlete in the history of American sport has been so widely commemorated and in so many different ways. At noon on May 4, 1972, there was a "Service of Thanksgiving and Commemoration for Robert Tyre Jones" at the Parish Church of Holy Trinity in St. Andrews. Roger Wethered, Jones' longtime friend and former competitor, gave the address: "To have won through at golf after those years

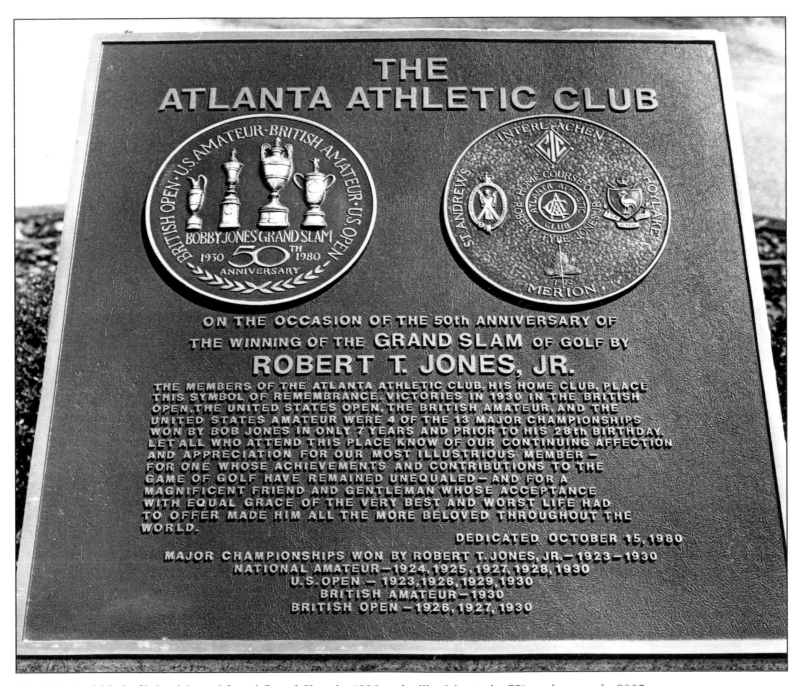

The Atlanta Athletic Club celebrated Jones' Grand Slam in 1980 and will celebrate the 75ᵗʰ anniversary in 2005.
Photo courtesy of the Atlanta Athletic Club.

1930s
CELEBRATE THE CENTURY™

Depression, Dust Bowl, and a New Deal

By 1933 the average wage was 60 percent less than in 1929 and unemployment had skyrocketed to 25 percent. Dust storms forced many farmers to give up their land.

Americans escaped harsh realities by playing Monopoly, reading the adventures of "Buck Rogers" and "Flash Gordon," and listening to Hoagy Carmichael's "Stardust." Popular films included *King Kong* and *It Happened One Night*. For the first time, African-American athletes became national idols: Joe Louis in boxing and Jesse Owens in track and field.

Prohibition was repealed in 1933. President Franklin Roosevelt fought the Great Depression with his New Deal programs. The "Star-Spangled Banner" was chosen as the national anthem. The Empire State Building rose above the Manhattan skyline and the Golden Gate Bridge spanned the San Francisco Bay. Back on the ground, the parking meter made its first appearance in 1935.

As the decade closed, many Americans were anxious about the growing war in Europe.

New words: all-star, oops, pizza, racism

COLLECT ALL TEN IN THE SERIES!
4 OF 10
PRICE: $4.80

The United States Postal Service has honored Bobby Jones with two stamps, the second in 1998.
Photo courtesy of the U.S. Postal Service.

when nothing would quite come right was an epic victory in itself, but the second victory—the one in which he was reduced to walking with difficulty with a cane and finally to a wheelchair—was a victory of the spirit that will also live as long as his name is remembered." The service, presided over by the Reverend C. Y. McGlashan, was arranged by the provost, magistrates, and councilors of the Royal Burgh of St. Andrews and the Royal and Ancient Golf Club of St. Andrews.

Ben Hogan once remarked that the "secret of Jones' success" was the "strength of the man's mind." No surprise, then, that Jones' name would become associated with intellectual enterprises. The Robert Tyre Jones Jr. Memorial Lecture on Legal Ethics at Emory University was inaugurated in 1974 by Justice Harry A. Blackmun of the United States Supreme Court and with the support of Jones' former law firm. An esteemed group participated in the series during its decade-long existence, including Blackmun, "Thoughts about Ethics" (1974–1975); Professor Paul A. Freund, "The Moral Education of the Lawyer" (1976–1977); and Alistair Cooke, "Ethics, Manners, and Sportsmanship" (1977–1978).

The evening before the final round of the 1976 U.S. Open at the Atlanta Athletic Club, an event that Jones helped secure before his death, the Memorial Arts Center in Atlanta (now the Woodruff Arts Center) hosted a celebration of Jones' legacy. USGA president Harry Easterly remarked: "What impresses me most is that it is now 46 years since the Grand Slam, and here we are gathering in a huge hall like this to honor Bob Jones." The same year as the Memorial Arts Center celebration, the Robert T.

Jones Jr. Scholarship Program was established by Emory University in Atlanta and the University of St. Andrews in Scotland as an exchange program to nurture college students who "possess the finest academic and personal qualifications."

F. M. "Buster" Bird, Jones' friend and former law partner, is credited with beginning the scholarship program in Jones' name. In 1977, a tax-deductible fund was established, and Bird in Atlanta, Joe Dey in New York, and Sir John Carmichael in Scotland became the guiding forces for the program. Today, Tom Cousins, Dick LeBlonde, and Sir Michael Bonnallack are at the helm. Each year, eight Jones Scholars are selected, four at each university. In addition, two or three graduate students from St. Andrews are offered an opportunity to study at an American university of their choice. The year-long scholarships, funded through three endowments, are intended to help foster the transatlantic ties that were so important to Jones.

A second scholarship program, established in 2002, provides for an exchange of graduate students between the University of St. Andrews and the Georgia Institute of Technology. The Robert T. Jones Jr. Fellowship program honors the Jones legacy at his undergraduate alma mater, Georgia Tech, where he received his bachelor of science degree in mechanical engineering in 1922, and the University of St. Andrews, located in his beloved city of St. Andrews, Scotland. The impetus for the establishment of the fellowship came from Charles R. Yates, a 1935 graduate of Georgia Tech, longtime secretary of Augusta National Golf Club, 1938 British Amateur champion, and friend of Bobby Jones. Funding for the support of the

Augusta National Golf Club cofounders Bobby Jones (left) and Clifford Roberts. Photo courtesy of the USGA.

fellowship is provided annually through the Robert T. Jones Jr. Memorial Scholarship Fund of New York.

On April 2, 1990, the Atlanta History Center hosted a Livingston Lecture Series titled "Bob Jones and the Early Days of The Masters," that featured Yates, who spoke about Jones' early years at East Lake and Augusta National Golf Club. Byron Nelson then analyzed Jones'

technique and described his own experience playing in The Masters. Finally, Cooke reflected on his memories of Jones. Five years later, the History Center opened a temporary exhibition, curated by Lynn Watson-Powers, titled *Robert Tyre Jones Jr.: Master Golfer* to showcase the Bob Jones collection that had recently been donated to the museum.

The 2004 Bobby Jones Scholars in period costume as extras for the film Bobby Jones—Stroke of Genius. Photo courtesy of Emory

Bobby Jones (left) with Ben Hogan at The Masters. Photo courtesy of the USGA.

The Atlanta Athletic Club hosted a program for both the 25th and 50th anniversaries of the Grand Slam and is hosting a similar celebration with the members of Merion, Interlachen, Hoylake, and the Royal and Ancient Golf Club of St. Andrews in September 2005 for the 75th anniversary. On March 17, 2002, on the 100th anniversary of Jones' birth, the Atlanta History Center collaborated with the Jones family and all of the organizations affiliated with his legacy to host a black-tie celebration honoring the centennial. Proceeds from that event help support the exhibition, Down the Fairway with Bobby Jones, and related programming. In May 2002, Peachtree Golf Club held a private celebration in honor of their former president and member.

For the past 25 years, the members of Merion Golf Club have honored Jones' victory at the 1930 U.S. Amateur on the last Friday in September. The course is closed to regular play, and a large group of members, averaging 75 each year, come together to remember Jones' accomplishment. They gather for lunch under a tent adjacent to the lower terrace and then play a ceremonial round of foursome golf, followed by a black-tie dinner. Before dinner, the members, led by a bagpiper, cross Ardmore Avenue to the tee box on the 11th hole to toast Bob Jones and his extraordinary achievement. They return to the club for a seafood buffet and a formal program. Past speakers have included Yates, Jim Dodson, and Jim Nantz. Members representing a variety of clubs, including the Atlanta Athletic Club, East Lake Golf Club, and Peachtree Golf Club, periodically participate as guests. In 1997, 44 players from overseas came to Merion for the event.

Dorothy and Charlie Yates at the 2002 Bobby Jones Centennial Dinner at the Atlanta History Center. Photo courtesy of the Atlanta History Center.

Bob Jones and the USGA
by Rand Jerris

From his first appearance in a USGA championship at the 1916 U.S. Amateur at Merion Cricket Club (now Merion Golf Club), Bob Jones enjoyed a special relationship with the USGA. Initially, it was the remarkable talents of the Atlanta teenager that captivated galleries and officials alike. But as Jones matured and learned to control his emotions, emerging as the outstanding player of his generation, it was his strength of character and his sportsmanship that earned him the respect of his peers.

It was no surprise, therefore, that Jones was nominated to serve on the USGA Executive Committee in 1928 at the age of 25, a position he would hold for three years. Unknown by many is the fact that Jones was a member of the Executive Committee at the time that he completed the Grand Slam in 1930. Following his retirement from competition shortly thereafter, Jones continued in his role as an important advisor and friend of the association. In 1955, the USGA established the Bob Jones Award—the association's highest honor—to recognize distinguished sportsmanship in golf. In 1937, Jones was nominated to serve as a member of the first USGA Museum and Library Committee. He would continue in this position until the time of his death in 1971, actively supporting the museum and its mission for almost 35 years.

Jones was a generous contributor to the museum, donating many celebrated artifacts from the most important moments in his career. In 1938, Jones presented to the USGA the putter—Calamity Jane II—that he used to win 10 of his 13 national championships. Three decades later, he donated his complete collection of U.S. Open, U.S. Amateur, British Open, British Amateur, and Walker Cup medals. Also included in the gift was the 1930 Sullivan Award, the first ever presented by the Amateur Athletic Union. In 1959, Jones was responsible for commissioning President Dwight D. Eisenhower to complete a painting of the 16th hole at Augusta National Golf Club. The painting is now one of the highlights of the museum's art collection.

Following Jones' passing in 1971, the Jones family continued its strong support of the museum and its mission, donating important collections of personal letters, photographs, and scrapbooks to the USGA archives. These and other treasures celebrating the life and career of golf's greatest amateur reside in the Bob Jones Room at Golf House. To commemorate the 75th anniversary of Bob Jones' Grand Slam, the USGA is both proud and honored to share the special artifacts with the Atlanta History Center and the people of Atlanta.

Since 1983, Highlands Country Club has hosted the Bob Jones Invitational, an annual golf tournament to benefit the Highland-Cashiers Hospital. The idea for the event is credited to Walter Wattles and Jim Mackey, who, at the time, was the president of the club. Located at the southern tip of the Blue Ridge Mountains, near the point where North Carolina, South Carolina, and Georgia meet, Highlands Country Club was one of the few places Jones could go to relax, away from the adoring crowds. Jones played it often and still holds the course record. The tournament is a way for the community to remember Jones, who maintained a summer home at the club. For the first six years, the tournament was a pro-am, featuring tour professionals such as Davis Love III and Ben Crenshaw matched with amateur golfers from the club and the community. The format was then changed to feature the American Walker Cup players. When the Walker Cup is played in the United States, several members of the Great Britain and Ireland team compete in the invitational as well. Played in the first or second week of August each year, the annual tournament is open to the public free of charge and features some of the best amateur golfers in the world.

Jones' legacy has grown exponentially since his death, and there are dozens of sites, in Atlanta and further afield, where his story is told. On December 30, 1933, the city of Atlanta dedicated the Bobby Jones Municipal Golf Course, an 18-hole course in Peachtree Battle Memorial Park that measured 6,423 yards and played to a par of 71. At 1:00 that afternoon, Jones hit the first ball and played in the first foursome with Yates, Billy Wilson, the professional at the Piedmont Park Municipal Golf Course, and Chick Ridley, former Georgia State Amateur champion.

The 145-acre site was transformed into one of the city's finest public courses, still very much in use today. It became the city's fifth municipal golf course.

Five miles from the Bobby Jones Golf Course, visitors to Atlanta will find Bobby Jones' gravesite. On December 20, 1971, he was buried in a small, private ceremony at Oakland Cemetery. Atlanta's oldest cemetery, established in 1850, Oakland is where visitors can see the graves of Margaret Mitchell, six Georgia governors, five Confederate generals, and prominent members of Atlanta's African-American and Jewish communities. In 1998, the nonprofit Imlay Foundation refurbished the site. The foundation hired a landscaping team to plant a horseshoe of the same 18 flowering trees that grace Augusta National's 18 holes. The gravesite itself is surrounded by pink roses, as well as golf balls and tees left by fans of the nation's most famous golfer. Each year, at Oakland's "Sunday in the Park" program in October, volunteers representing the Atlanta History Center are on hand to interpret Jones' gravesite; each year the crowds grow larger.

While Jones has been inducted into half a dozen athletic and golf halls of fame, museums and private golf clubs throughout the United States and Britain have played a critical role in preserving his legacy. Golf House, opened in 1972 at the headquarters of the United States Golf Association in Far Hills, New Jersey, has a Bob Jones Room that documents his stunning career and features 32 tournament medals, a photographic history of the Grand Slam, manuscripts, and his famous putter, Calamity Jane II, which is mounted below his portrait. With the assistance of Rand Jerris and Nancy Stulack of the USGA, the Jones Collection will be on display for the Grand Slam

ROBERT TYRE JONES JR.,

MASTER GOLFER:

*An Exhibition of
the Bob Jones Collection*

ATLANTA
HISTORY
CENTER

DOWN THE FAIRWAY WITH

Bobby Jones

on exhibit at the

ATLANTA HISTORY CENTER

SCORE AN EAGLE WHEN YOU VISIT

$2 off one general admission to the
Atlanta History Center with this card

The Atlanta History Center has hosted two exhibitions on Jones. Photos courtesy of the Atlanta History Center.

The Atlanta Athletic Club's homage to their most famous member. Photo courtesy of the Atlanta Athletic Club.

year at the Atlanta History Center. The USGA's photo archives and library also contain extensive manuscript and photograph holdings related to Jones' life. Augusta National Golf Club is home to Calamity Jane I, which is part of a small but impressive collection of Jones materials related to his years as a competitor and his longtime relationship to the club and The Masters.

The Atlanta Athletic Club's Bobby Jones Memorial Room, opened in time for the 1976 U.S. Open hosted by the club, includes a diverse collection of Jones' trophies

Bobby Jones (right) with Dave Estes, head of Special Collections at Emory University in the late sixties. Photo courtesy of Special Collections, Robert W. Woodruff Library, Emory University.

"Perhaps it is best simply to say there was a touch of poetry to his golf, so there was always a certain, definite magic about the man himself."

—HERBERT WARREN WIND

and memorabilia. For the opening, the USGA loaned the club the Eisenhower Trophy and the Walker Cup. The club recently cataloged its archival collection, making manuscripts, photographs, and artifacts related to Jones and his home club available to researchers. East Lake Golf Club houses an important collection of golfing memorabilia from the golden age of American sports, as well as a small archive. The British Golf Museum in St. Andrews, Scotland, under the direction of Peter Lewis, documents the history of Jones' amateur career in its exhibition that spans five hundred years of golf history. The Special Collections Department at the Robert W. Woodruff Library of Emory University has a large Bobby Jones manuscript collection that contains letters, news clippings, plaques, and photographs. A small case of artifacts documenting Jones, one of the university's most famous students, is on display in the library's reading room.

The most comprehensive exhibition on Jones, though, is at the Atlanta History Center. Down the Fairway with Bobby Jones, the largest permanent exhibition on Jones in a public institution, opened on April 5, 1999. The Bob Jones Collection came to the Atlanta History Center in 1994 when a group of local business leaders and foundations, led by Cousins, Imlay, William L. O'Callaghan, Allen W. Post Jr., Robert M. Varn, and Yates, joined together to purchase and donate Jones' historic artifacts. In 1997, Dr. Catherine Lewis began working on the exhibit, which examines the origins of the game, the growth of specific courses and clubs in the Gilded Age, the rise of public courses, golf course desegregation, the growing professionalization of golf, and the meaning of golf and sport in American culture. Divided into three thematic sections ("The Early History of

The Jones family, with Dr. Catherine Lewis (second from right) and executive director Rick Beard (far right), at the 2002 Bobby Jones Centennial Dinner at the Atlanta History Center. Photo courtesy of the Atlanta History Center.

A poster advertising Bobby Jones—Stroke of Genius.
Photo courtesy of Kim Dawson.

Golf," "The Age of the Amateur," and "The Making of the Modern Game"), the exhibition analyzes Jones' career within broader themes of sports history. To supplement the exhibition, the Atlanta History Center's Kenan Research Center also has a large archival collection related to Jones and the history of golf and is home to Jones' private library, part of the original Bob Jones Collection.

In addition to celebrations, scholarships, and exhibitions, Jones has been the subject of books, articles, newsreels, and feature films. His likeness has appeared on everything from Coca-Cola advertisements to golf shirts. In the past decade, dozens of writers and historians have published books to analyze his role in the history of sports. In 1930, the year Jones retired, a Hollywood producer approached Jones about starring in a film titled *Follow Through*, but he wisely refused. More recently, Hollywood has rediscovered Jones. Two feature films have included Jones as a main character, cementing his status as a cultural icon for a new generation. *The Legend of Bagger Vance* was released in 2000. On April 30, 2004, the second film, *Bobby Jones—Stroke of Genius*, opened. The project, which took 13 years to complete, was completed in collaboration with the St. Andrews Links Trust and Augusta National Golf Club. This was the first film to gain permission to shoot at both of the fabled golf courses. Nine other golf courses in Atlanta were used to represent various competition sites, including the public Bobby Jones Golf Course and the courses at Château Élan, north of the city. To give back to the game, the producers established the Bobby Jones Film Foundation and made a donation to the Atlanta History Center, the First Tee, and the Robert T. Jones Jr. Scholarship Program.

The past two decades have seen a proliferation of books on Jones' career and legacy. Between Jones' death in 1971 and 1997, 18 books appeared on him. In the last five years alone, nearly 20 more have been published. This outpouring of biographies of and scholarly monographs on him indicates that interest in him has not diminished.

The federal government also has played a role in disseminating Jones' legacy. The United States Postal Service has honored Jones three times, once with a temporary post office named for his famous putter and twice with stamps. In 1976, to coincide with the U.S. Open hosted by the Atlanta Athletic Club, J. Heard Summerour, the postmaster of Duluth, Georgia, proposed the idea of building a temporary post office near the first tee of the Highlands course. The Calamity Jane Post Office was used exclusively by ticketholders during the week of the championship. In 1981, on the 10th anniversary of Jones' death, a commemorative stamp was issued. The Postal Service released a second stamp on August 27, 1998, as part of its "Celebrate the Century" series.

Today's fans who want to know Bobby Jones can turn on the Golf Channel, watch The Masters broadcast on CBS, log on to the Internet, or take a trip to an upscale mall or country club. During his lifetime, Jones lent his name to only one company—A. G. Spalding and Brothers in 1932 to promote his matched set of steel-shafted irons. That license expired sometime in the fifties, and his name was not used for three decades. Today, four companies—Bobby Jones Sportswear, Golf Links to the Past, Inc., Bobby Jones Golf, and Bobby Jones Productions—have made it their business to promote Jones under the Bobby Jones brand, closely moni-

tored by the Jones family, represented by Martin J. Elgison of Jones' former law firm.

In October 2004, Bobby Jones Productions, the fourth and the newest of the Jones licensees, reintroduced the 18 short films that Jones made in the thirties. Though the films were part of the Warner Brothers library, they were not widely available until the advent of home video in the eighties. Peachtree Golf Club had a copy that it would periodically show to members as part of a social program, and WGTV in Atlanta showed the series in 1975, but the films essentially were unavailable to the public. In 1986, Turner Broadcasting System purchased Warner Brothers' pre-1948 library, which includes the Jones films, as well as classics such as *Casablanca, Citizen Kane, Gone with the Wind, The Wizard of Oz,* and *King Kong.*

Ely Callaway, the founder of Callaway Golf, played an important role in reintroducing the films. Callaway convinced Steve Chamberlain, who oversaw the Turner library and was responsible for the distribution of the films worldwide in home video, to license the films to him and to SyberVision, a company that specialized in sports instruction. Callaway saw the potential of using Bobby Jones to help market Callaway Golf and a boutique set of golf clubs bearing the Jones name. Late in 1986, SyberVision released a VHS set that included a book, two VHS cassettes, and a certificate of authenticity. More than fifty thousand copies eventually were sold, more than any other instructional series on golf to date. The company later edited the 18 films into a shorter program that focused on the long game, short game, and a complete round of golf. In the late nineties, SyberVision experienced financial difficulties and sublicensed the Bobby

Alexa Stirling Fraser, a childhood friend of Bobby Jones, opening the Bobby Jones Room at the Atlanta Athletic Club in 1976.
Photo courtesy of the Atlanta Athletic Club.

Jones series to Best Video. Though used copies of the VHS series are still available via the Internet, Best Video's license expired and the instructional series went out of print in 2002. In 2004, Chamberlain met with executives at Turner Entertainment Company (a division of Time Warner) and the Jones family to establish a longterm licensing agreement to rerelease the films under Chamberlain's company, Bobby Jones Productions. Unlike the SyberVision version, the new series used digital versatile disc (DVD) technology, which improved the quality of the sound and picture, thus contributing to the preservation of the original films. Two versions, the Collectors

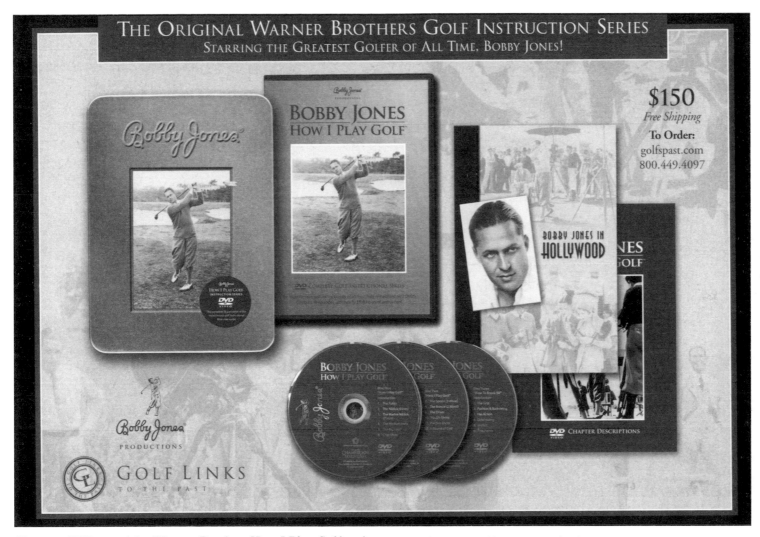

The new DVD set of the Warner Brothers How I Play Golf *series.* Photo courtesy of Bobby Jones Productions.

Edition and the Complete Golf Instructional Series Edition, are currently available.

In 2005, on the 75th anniversary of the Grand Slam, the golfing world will once again focus on Jones and his extraordinary accomplishment. The Atlanta History Center, in partnership with the Jones family, the United States Golf Association, the Atlanta Athletic Club, Merion Golf Club, and the R&A will create a traveling exhibition that analyzes and celebrates the event. It will open officially at the Atlanta History Center for its annual fundraising event, the Swan House Ball, on April 30. The exhibition will travel to the U.S. Open at Pinehurst, the British Open at the Old Course in St. Andrews, the U.S. Amateur at Merion, the Atlanta Athletic Club's celebration of the 75th anniversary of the Grand Slam in September and October, and finally to the Tour Championship at East Lake.

Additionally, throughout 2005, the USGA will loan the Bobby Jones Collection to the Atlanta History Center. The artifacts, including Calamity Jane II, Jones' competition medals, and his 1930 passport, will be integrated into Down the Fairway with Bobby Jones, the History Center's signature exhibition on his life and legacy. The exhibition, without artifacts, will then travel for the next 10 years to schools, tournaments, libraries, and community centers. This project will give a new generation plenty of opportunities to acquaint themselves with the Bobby Jones story.

What attracts people to the Jones legacy today is the same thing that made Jones appealing during his competitive career that ended in 1930. He played golf for the sheer joy and friendships it brought him, even though it sometimes frustrated him. His battle with his temper and ultimate mastery of it reflected how much passion he felt for the game and competition at the highest level. He played golf as well as anyone ever has; he conducted himself as a gentleman on and off the course; and the stature of his achievements will continue to endure.

"When one plays against Mr. Jones, he has only the pleasure of being defeated by the greatest of all golfers and the finest of all sportsmen."

—T. PHILIP PERKINS

Bob Jones Award Winners

In 1955, the United States Golf Association established the Bob Jones Award to honor a person who, by a single act or over the years, emulated Jones' sportsmanship, respect for the game and its rules, generosity of spirit, sense of fair play, and perhaps even sacrifice. In 1966, Jones reflected in an article for the *Atlanta Journal* that "[t]he quality of sportsmanship is the quality I would most want to be praised for."

From left: Bobby Jones, Ike Grainger, and 1955 Bob Jones Award recipient Francis Ouimet. Photo courtesy of the USGA.

1955 Francis D. Ouimet
1956 William C. Campbell
1957 Mildred D. Zaharias
1958 Margaret Curtis
1959 Findlay S. Douglas
1960 Charles "Chick" Evans Jr.
1961 Joseph B. Carr
1962 Horton Smith
1963 Patty Berg
1964 Charles R. Coe
1965 Glenna Collett Vare
1966 Gary Player
1967 Richard S. Tufts
1968 Robert B. Dickson
1969 Gerald H. Micklem
1970 Roberto de Vicenzo
1971 Arnold Palmer
1972 Michael Bonallack

1973 Gene Littler
1974 Byron Nelson
1975 Jack Nicklaus
1976 Ben Hogan
1977 Joseph C. Dey Jr.
1978 Bing Crosby and Bob Hope
1979 Tom Kite
1980 Charles R. Yates
1981 JoAnne Gunderson Carner
1982 William J. Patton
1983 Maureen Ruttle Garrett
1984 R. Jay Sigel
1985 Fuzzy Zoeller
1986 Jess W. Sweetser
1987 Tom Watson
1988 Isaac B. Grainger
1989 Chi Chi Rodriguez
1990 Peggy Kirk Bell

1991 Ben Crenshaw
1992 Gene Sarazen
1993 P. J. Boatwright Jr.
1994 Lewis Oehmig
1995 Herbert Warren Wind
1996 Betsy Rawls
1997 Fred Brand Jr.
1998 Nancy Lopez
1999 Ed Updegraff
2000 Barbara McIntire
2001 Thomas Cousins
2002 Judy Rankin
2003 Carol Semple Thompson
2004 Jack Burke Jr.
2005 Nick Price

Appendix I

*Further Information about the Atlanta
History Center, R&A, and USGA
Museum and Archives*

In 2005 the Atlanta History Center will coordinate the celebration to honor the 75th anniversary of Bobby Jones' Grand Slam, one of the most memorable moments in the history of golf in the 20th century. This book will accompany a traveling exhibition created by the Atlanta History Center, also titled Bobby Jones and the Quest for the Grand Slam, in collaboration with the Jones family, the United States Golf Association, the R&A, Merion Golf Club, and the Atlanta Athletic Club. The exhibition will premier at the Atlanta History Center's Swan House Ball in April, and will then travel to the United States Open at Pinehurst in June, the British Open at St. Andrews in July, the U.S. Open at Merion Golf Club in August, the Atlanta Athletic Club's 75th anniversary celebration in September, and the Tour Championship at East Lake Golf Club in November. It will be seen by nearly 1 million people and continue to travel for the next 10 years.

The Atlanta History Center

*Atlanta History Center
130 W. Paces Ferry Road, NW
Atlanta, GA 30305-1366
404-814-4000
www.atlantahistorycenter.com*

Founded as the Atlanta Historical Society in 1926, the Atlanta History Center is proud to offer historical perspectives for all ages, integrating history, education and life-enrichment programs at its campus located in Atlanta. As a historical and educational venue specializing in southern history and culture, Atlanta History Center offerings include the thirty thousand–square-foot Atlanta History Museum, featuring four signature exhibitions and two galleries for traveling exhibitions.

Signature exhibitions focus on key events, places, and people in southern history. The most recent signature exhibition focuses on Bobby Jones. From the phenomenal story of one of the greatest golf legends to the rolling green fairways of Augusta National and The Masters, Georgia has led the way in the development of golf as one of the nation's best-loved sports. The exhibit Down the Fairway with Bobby Jones traces Georgia's involvement in golf from course development and tournament play to the introduction of women into the game and the integration of public courses. At the center of the exhibition is the story of the man considered to be the most important golfer in the history of the sport— Bobby Jones. Photographs and personal artifacts follow his life through his incomparable number of tournament wins, family ties, successful business career, and dedication to golf. Other sections, including "Early History of the Game," "Age of the Amateur," and "The Modern Era," feature unique items such as an 1840s feathery ball, golf clubs from the 18th century, replicas of Jones' four Grand Slam trophies, rule books from St. Andrews in Scotland, golf clothing and shoes, a coveted Masters' green jacket, original papers from desegregation proceedings, scorecards, badges, and junior golf artifacts. In 1999–2000, the Georgia Association of Museums and Galleries recognized Down the Fairway with Bobby Jones as the best permanent exhibition in Georgia. In 2000, Dr. Catherine Lewis, the exhibition curator, published *Considerable Passions: Golf, the Masters, and the Legacy of Bobby Jones* to accompany the exhibition.

The R&A

British Golf Museum
Bruce Embankment
St. Andrews, Fife KY16 9AB
01334 460064
www.britishgolfmuseum.co.uk

The R&A takes its name from the Royal and Ancient Golf Club of St Andrews, which traces its origins back 250 years. The R&A has grown apart from the golf club to focus on its role as golf's world governance and development body and organizer of the Open Championship.

The R&A is the trust-owned sports business behind the Open, golf's biggest major, and the international organization that maintains the Rules of Golf. All of this work is carried out with the consent of 125 national and international amateur and professional organizations from 110 countries on behalf of an estimated 26 million golfers in Europe, Africa, Asia, and the Americas (outside the USA and Mexico). The United States Golf Association (USGA) is the game's governing body in the United States and Mexico. The R&A and the USGA have jointly issued the Rules of Golf since 1952.

By making the Open Championship one of the world's great sporting events and an outstanding commercial success, the R&A is able to invest a substantial annual surplus for the development of the game. The R&A Foundation is the charitable body that channels money from the Open directly into grassroots development projects around the world. Particular emphasis is placed on the encouragement of junior golf, on the development of the game in emerging golfing nations, on coaching and the provision of more accessible courses, and improved practice facilities. The R&A provides guidance on all aspects of golf course management to help golf grow throughout the world in a commercially and environmentally sustainable way.

The R&A continues to uphold a commitment to the game's heritage that began in 1864. In 1987, the Royal and Ancient Golf Club established a charitable trust to create and run the British Golf Museum. Part of the purpose of setting up the museum was to allow much of the club's collection of balls, trophies, clubs, and memorabilia to be seen on public display. The British Golf Museum opened to great critical acclaim in June 1990. The museum tells the story of the history of golf in Britain from the Middle Ages to the present day, and of British influence abroad.

The United States Golf Association Museum and Archives

United States Golf Association Museum and Archives
77 Liberty Corner Road
Far Hills, NJ 07931
908-234-2300
museum@usga.org
www.usga.org

The United States Golf Association has served as the national governing body of golf since its formation in 1894. It is a nonprofit organization run by golfers for the benefit of golfers, committed to promoting policies and programs for the good of the game. The association provides essential services for all golfers, whether they are amateurs or professionals, public or private course players. Among its most important functions, the USGA, together with the R&A in St. Andrews, Scotland, writes and interprets the Rules of Golf. The USGA also conducts golf's national championships, including the U.S. Open, U.S. Women's Open, U.S. Senior Open, 10 national amateur championships, and the State Team Championships. In addition, the USGA produces the Rules of Amateur Status, funds turf-grass and environmental research, formulates a national handicap system, maintains equipment standards, and ensures the future of the game through its Grants and Fellowship Program.

The USGA comprises more than nine thousand private and public courses, clubs, and facilities. An executive committee of 15 volunteers oversees the association. More than thirteen hundred volunteers from all parts of the country also serve on other USGA committees. A professional staff of approximately 350 directs the association's day-to-day functions from Golf House, the USGA's headquarters in Far Hills, New Jersey.

Founded in 1935, the USGA Museum and Archives is the oldest museum dedicated to sports in the United States. Since the USGA began collecting historical materials, the collections have grown to encompass more than forty-two thousand artifacts, a library of more than twenty thousand volumes, more than half a million photographic images, and several thousand hours of film and video footage. The USGA Museum is now home to the premier collection of golf memorabilia in the world.

Among the many treasures in the collections, one may find more than 400 clubs and balls used by USGA champions, the golf club (actually, a modified soil sampling tool) used by Alan Shepard to hit golf balls on the surface of the moon in 1971, the gold medal awarded to the first U.S. Open Champion, Horace Rawlins, in 1895, and the workbench and tools of an early 20th-century Scottish clubmaker. The collections also contain a multitude of personal items from golf's greatest legends, including Bob Jones, Gene Sarazen, Walter Hagen, Byron Nelson, Ben Hogan, Patty Berg, Babe Zaharias, Arnold Palmer, Jack Nicklaus, and Tiger Woods. In their depth, breadth, and quality, these collections reflect the USGA's commitment to preserving and promoting the traditions and history of the game.

Appendix II

Timeline

1902—Robert Tyre "Bobby" Jones Jr. is born on March 17 to Robert P. and Clara Jones in the Atlanta neighborhood of Grant Park.

1908—At age six, Jones competes in his first tournament, at East Lake. Although technically defeated by Alexa Stirling, he is awarded the trophy.

1916—At age 14, Jones wins the Georgia State Amateur Championship, defeating Perry Adair. He also travels to the Merion Cricket Club near Philadelphia to become the youngest competitor in the U.S. Amateur; he loses in the third round to Bob Gardner. During what sportswriter O. B. Keeler labeled the "Seven Lean Years," Jones plays in dozens of tournaments but is unable to capture a major championship.

1917—Jones becomes the youngest player ever to win the Southern Amateur. Jones plays in numerous exhibition events with fellow young golfers Perry Adair, Alexa Stirling, and Elaine Rosenthal, raising more than $150,000 for the American Red Cross World War I relief effort.

1921—On June 25, during the third round of the British Open, Jones loses his temper and disqualifies himself from the tournament. Both Jones and historians mark this as the most "transcendent moment of his golfing career."

1922—Jones, who graduated from Atlanta's Tech High School at 16, completes his bachelor of science degree in mechanical engineering at the Georgia Institute of Technology.

1923—Jones wins his first major championship, the U.S. Open, at Inwood Country Club in New York. He beats Bobby Cruickshank in a playoff, thus ending the "Seven Lean Years."

1924—Jones wins the U.S. Amateur at Merion Cricket Club (now Merion Golf Club) in Ardmore, Pennsylvania, defeating George Von Elm, 9 and 8, in the final round. Jones receives a degree in English literature from Harvard. On June 17 he marries Mary Rice Malone in Atlanta. They eventually have three children: Clara, Robert Tyre Jones III, and Mary Ellen.

1925—Jones wins the U.S. Amateur at Oakmont Country Club in Pennsylvania, defeating fellow East Lake golfer Watts Gunn, 8 and 7, on the 29th hole. This is the only time two members of the same club have met in the finals of a major championship.

1926—Jones wins his first British Open at Royal Lytham and St. Anne's. He hits what has been called "the greatest shot in the history of British golf" on the 17th hole to pull ahead of American professional Al Watrous. Jones was the first American amateur to win the Open. Jones becomes the first golfer to win the "double"—the U.S. Open and the British Open—in a single season, by winning the U.S. Open at Scioto Country Club in Columbus, Ohio. He went into the final hole tied with Joe Turnesa, but birdied the hole to win the Open by a stroke.

1927—Jones publishes *Down the Fairway* in collaboration with O. B. Keeler, an *Atlanta Journal* sportswriter and Bobby Jones' "secret weapon." Jones successfully defends his British Open championship at the Old Course in St. Andrews, Scotland. Jones wins the U.S. Amateur at the Minikhada Club in Minneapolis, defeating Chick Evans, 8 and 7, on the 29th hole of the 36-hole final.

1928—After little more than one year at Emory University Law School, Jones passes the state bar exam. On January 13 he is admitted to the Georgia Bar and enters his father's law firm. Jones wins his fourth U.S. Amateur by defeating T. Philip Perkins, 10 and 9, at the Brae Burn Country Club near Boston.

1929—Jones wins the U.S. Open at Winged Foot Golf Club in Mamaroneck, New York. Going to the 17th hole during the last round, Jones needed two pars just to force a playoff. He got his par and pitched onto the 18th green, leaving him with a difficult putt to tie. He made the putt, forcing a 36-hole playoff with Al Espinosa. He dominated the playoff and defeated Espinosa by 23 strokes.

1930—Jones captains the American Walker Cup team, played at the Royal St. George's Golf Club in Sandwich, England. The team went on to win the Cup 10 to 2. Jones plays in what he terms "the most important tournament of my life," the 1930 British Amateur at St. Andrews. He defeats Roger Wethered on the 13th hole of the second 18 to win his first and only British Amateur. Jones goes to Hoylake, England, to play in the British Open at the Royal Liverpool Golf Club. After the second round, Jones was a stroke ahead. He struggled in the third round and shot a 2-over-par 74. He shot a 75 in the fourth round to hold on for the win. Shortly after his triumphant return from Britain, Jones heads to the Interlachen Country Club in Minneapolis for the U.S. Open. Jones shot a 1-under-par 71 in the first round to stay one behind the leaders. He finished the second round at 73-even par for the tournament and 2 strokes off the lead. He then played an outstanding third round, shooting 68 to give himself a 5-stroke lead going into the fourth, and an erratic fourth round, making three double bogeys and three birdies on the way to a 3-over-par 75. Jones waited more than an hour while Macdonald Smith, his closest pursuer, finished 2 strokes back, giving Jones his fourth U.S. Open championship. Jones returns to Merion, the site of his first U.S. Amateur competition and his first win in the U.S. Amateur, to try to complete the Grand Slam of golf. During the finals, marines were brought out to help control the huge crowds that were grabbing at Jones. He won the qualifying medal and the "Impregnable Quadrilateral of Golf," also known as the Grand Slam. On November 13 Jones signs a con-

tract with Warner Brothers to make a series of one-reel motion pictures devoted entirely to golf instruction. On November 17 Bobby Jones announces his retirement from golf.

1932—Augusta National Golf Club, designed by Bobby Jones and Dr. Alister MacKenzie, is completed in December and opens for play the following month.

1933—On December 30, the city of Atlanta dedicates the Bobby Jones Municipal Golf Course, an 18-hole course in Peachtree Battle Memorial Park that measured 6,423 yards and played to a par of 71.

1934—The First Annual Invitational Tournament, now known as The Masters, is played in March at Augusta National.

1942—On June 9 Jones is commissioned as a captain in the Army Air Force. A medical disability and his age (40) does not compel him to go to war, but he insists upon serving. He is honorably discharged in August 1944.

1948—Peachtree Golf Club, an Atlanta course designed by Robert Trent Jones and Bobby Jones, opens. Owing to poor health, Jones plays his last round of golf at East Lake with Bob Ingram, Tommy Barnes, and Henry Lindner.

1955—Jones is diagnosed with syringomyelia, a degenerative spinal disease. That same year the United States Golf Association establishes the annual Bob Jones Award, honoring a person who, by a single act or over the years, emulates Jones' sportsmanship, respect for the game and its rules, generosity of spirit, sense of fair play, self-control, and perhaps even sacrifice. The award's first recipient is Francis Ouimet.

1958—The people of St. Andrews confer the Freedom of the City and the Royal Burgh of St. Andrews on Jones. The only other American ever so honored was Benjamin Franklin in 1759.

1960—Jones publishes *Golf Is My Game*

1966—Jones publishes *Bobby Jones on Golf*.

1969—Jones publishes *Bobby Jones on the Basic Golf Swing*.

1971—Bobby Jones dies on December 18 and is buried in Atlanta's Oakland Cemetery. On this day, golfers at St. Andrews stopped their play and the flag at the clubhouse was lowered to half-mast.

1972—On July 20 Jones is inducted into the Southern Golf Hall of Fame. After a memorial service on September 10 at Trinity Church, the 10th hole at the Old Course at St. Andrews is named in honor of Bobby Jones.

1976—Atlanta's Emory University establishes the Bobby Jones Scholarship Program, a scholarship exchange program with St. Andrews University in Scotland.

1981—A commemorative Bobby Jones stamp is issued by the U.S. Postal Service.

1983—Highlands Country Club begins hosting the Bob Jones Invitational, an annual golf tournament to benefit the Highland-Cashiers Hospital.

1988—Bobby Jones Sportswear, a luxury clothing line carrying the Jones name, is established as a division of Hickey Freeman.

1989—On January 14 Bobby Jones is inducted into the Georgia Golf Hall of Fame.

1995—Golf Links to the Past, Inc., the licensee for golf collectibles carrying Jones' likeness, is established.

1998—A second commemorative stamp is issued as part of the U.S. Postal Service's "Celebrate the Century" series.

1999—Down the Fairway with Bobby Jones, the only permanent exhibition on Jones' life and legacy, opens at the Atlanta History Center.

2000—*The Legend of Bagger Vance* featuring Bobby Jones as a character is released in theaters.

2002—The Georgia Institute of Technology establishes the Robert T. Jones Jr. Fellowship for an exchange of graduate students between the University of St. Andrews and Georgia Tech.

2004—On April 30, *Bobby Jones—Stroke of Genius*, a film on Jones' life and legacy, is released to a national audience, and Bobby Jones Productions reintroduces the 18 short films that Jones made in the thirties.

2005—At the PGA Merchandise Show in Orlando, Florida, the Bobby Jones Golf Company introduces a new line of golf clubs bearing the Jones name. On the 75th anniversary of the Grand Slam, the Atlanta History Center in partnership with the Jones family, the United States Golf Association, the Atlanta Athletic Club, Merion Golf Club, the R&A, and the British Golf Museum, coordinates the 75th anniversary celebration of the Grand Slam, featuring a traveling exhibition.

Appendix III
Bobby Jones Scolars,
Fellowships, and Scholarships

Bobby Jones Scholars

Year	*University of St. Andrews*	*Emory University*
1976–1977	David Marshall	Duncan Rennie
1977–1978	Lyman H. Reynolds Jr.	David N. M. Caborn
	Hugh S. Worsham	Gordon Muir-Carby
1978–1979	Anne Hill Barry	Sheena F. Gardner
	Samuel J. Durham	Alistair Michael Hicks
	Philip B. Paty Jr.	Carole Riley
1979–1980	Andrew Charles Adank	Colin Kerr Archibald
	Steven C. Andrews	Christopher G. Barr
	George W. Fryhofer III	Lindsay Joan MacGregor
	Caren Gaines Wilkie	Joanna Louise Marston
1980–1981	Leonard Leslie Bessant	Andrew J. Q. Church
	Helene B. Greenwald	Michael David Graham
	William R. Richardson	Mark Mullins
	Gary Spear	Fiona Jayne Smith
1981–1982	Steven L. Brown	Donald James Galbraith
	David O. Compton Jr.	Amanda Ridings
	Lisa Lawley	Andrew Rushton
	Charles L. Scott	Valerie Ann Sanderson
1982–1983	Deborah Genzer	Paul Logan
	Jan Gurley	Sally Knatchbull-Hugessen O'Brien
	Maeve A. Howett	Hamish Wilson Taylor
	John Edward McEachern	Alan Thomson

Year	*University of St. Andrews*	*Emory University*
1983–1984	Jill Elaine Bouma	Charles A. Bleau
	David W. Henry	Sally Burtles
	Renelda E. Mack	Lilias Graham
	David F. Moore	Peter Liney
1984–1985	Patricia Armstrong	Catriona Barr
	Michael Diehl	Thomas J. Linton
	Polly Price	Andrew J. M. Smith
	Timothy Whitehouse	Amanda Spafford
1985–1986	Susan C. Duhig	Douglas A. Currie
	Thomas C. Kruse	S. Alexander Haslam
	Georgia A. Popplewell	Ulrike R. M. Hellen
	Chris Schoettle	Brian Viner
1986–1987	Miriam C. Davis	Susan M. Allan
	Gail Goldsmith	Nicholas H. Barker
	Charles M. Grant	Zoe Day
	Lee F. Silverberg	Luke L. Porter
1987–1988	Steven Mitchell Cannon	Denise Ann Dawson
	Jeffrey Allen Smith	Donald H. M. Farquharson
	Adam E. Sohnen	Julia Helen Parry
	K. Eric Wommack	David Cameron Thaw
1988–1989	Michaele Bruzzese	Seymour P. M. Banks
	Jeffrey C. Kishpaugh	Gillian A. M. Kellock
	Maria Salterio	Douglas J. Russell
	Jennifer Untz Lee	Victoria E. Stanhope
1989–1990	Brian Charles Barlow	Rachel Cacanas
	Edward Robertson Mallard	Vivienne Musgrave
	Ayman Naseri	Maxine Pritchard
	Eric Arden Youngstrom	David Walker

Year	University of St. Andrews	Emory University
1990–1991	Scott F. Bertschi	Duncan Forbes
	Frederick Ming Chen	Jonathon Ledgard
	Paul Entis	Tim Medlock
	Shannan Ford LaPorte	Elizabeth Pharoah
1991–1992	Lisa Kung	Tracey Horn
	Neha Harish Mehta	Will Lane
	Shawn Robinson	Catriona MacDonald
	Stephen Bruce Tackney	Nicola Ward
1992–1993	Elizabeth Elliott	Duncan Castles
	Kwame J. Lawson	Gregor Findlay
	Edward Andre Nahmias	Anna McKenzie
	Adam Louis Silverman	Jennifer Murray
1993–1994	Chris Caplinger	Caroline Irving
	Jonathan Lass	Sara Lilliedal-Brown
	Gabrielle Starr	Ramsey Mirza
	Ron Wilder	Elizabeth Quigley
1994–1995	Lorri Hewett	James C. Albrecht
	Kristen Horton	Stuart J. Freeman
	Bernadette May-Beaver	Eileen M. McGowne
	Mark Richardson	Catriona M. Moore
1995–1996	Bimal Ramesh Desai	Jacqueline Cassidy
	Keri Eisenbeis	Lyndsay Mowat
	Barry Kendall	Katherine Orr
	David Kirkpatrick	Elizabeth Wilson
1996–1997	Holly Gregory	Paul Grogan
	Christopher Nunn	Debra Loney
	Katherine Wilson	Colin Spurway
	Sarah Zeff	Andrew White
1997–1998	Megan Bern	Gavin Bushell
	Daniel Colman	Prune Harris
	Lan Nguyen	Gail Richardson
	Michele Santamaria	Gavin Smith

Year	*University of St. Andrews*	*Emory University*
1998–1999	Justin Biel	Vincent Barnes
	Lakshmi Gopal	Lucy MacIntyre
	Jehangir Malegam	Deborah Palmer
	Rachel Park Haws	Graeme Young
1999–2000	Andrew Dober	Donald Lowe
	Robert (Jack) Casey	Caroline McDonald
	Lewis Satterwhite	Jenny Marra
	Anna Wheeler	Fiona Morris
2000–2001	Stuart Ambrose	Catherine Callard
	Kelly Healy	Tom Campbell
	Kathleen Jones	Gordon Fernie
	Marcus Moore	Megan Fisher
2001–2002	J. C. Aevaliotis	Kirsty Hunter
	Heather McCaffrey	Jamie Livingstone
	Jonathan Travis Sentell	Jessica Milligan
	Elizabeth Smith	Matthew Moore
2002–2003	Elizabeth Barchas	Mark MacLeod
	William Leasure	Joanne Stoddart
	Lauren Mayros	Caroline Kerr Thorpe
	David Roemer	Claire Lara Kyriakides-Yeldham
2003–2004	Dylan Bird	Christopher Dale
	Joel Boggan	Tim Hayden-Smith
	Melissa Roberts	Rob Huddart
	Kyle Wamstad	Beth Lynch
2004–2005	Euler Bropleh	Annette Jeneson
	Emily Hunter	Derek MacLeod
	Josh McCaleb	Alison Pollard
	Pete Sherlock	Ben Spiers

Robert T. Jones Jr. Fellowship at Georgia Institute of Technology

2002–2003

- David Gherardi—BS physics 2002, University of St. Andrews; MS electrical and computer engineering, Georgia Institute of Technology 2003
- Jason Beebe—BS physics, Georgia Institute of Technology 2002; MSc in photonics and optoelectronic devices, St. Andrews 2003

2003–2004

- Stephen Moore—BS physics 2003, University of St. Andrews; MS electrical and computer engineering, Georgia Institute of Technology 2004
- Elisa Hurwitz—BS electrical and computer engineering, Georgia Institute of Technology 2002; MSc in photonics and optoelectronic devices, Heriott Watt 2003

2004–2005

- David Thomas—BS physics 2004, University of St. Andrews
- Barry Mullins—BS electical and computer engineering, Georgia Institute of Technology 2002

Emory University Committee for the Robert Tyre Jones Jr. Scholarship

Committee

James H. Blanchard, chairman

Sir Michael Bonallack

David E. Boyd

Thomas G. Cousins

Bradley Currey Jr.

Martin J. Elgison

William H. Fox

James R. Griggs

Linton C. Hopkins III

Arthur Howell

John P. Imlay Jr.

Warren Y. Jobe

Ben F. Johnson III

Joseph W. Jones

Brian Lang

Richard K. LeBlond II

William O'Callaghan Jr.

Richard M. Olnick

Polly Price

J. Neal Purcell

James M. Sibley

Martin Van Buren Teem Jr.

James W. Wagner

Charles R. Yates

Charles R. Yates Jr.

University of St. Andrews Committee for the Robert Tyre Jones Jr. Scholarship

Trustees

Sir Michael Bonallack, chairman

C. Blake

Sir Philip Cohen

A. R. Cole-Hamilton

W. G. Davidson

B. Lang

J. C. McInnes

C. J. R. Philip

Ms. A. Ridings

G. M. Simmers

R. S. Waddell

Robert T. Jones Jr. Memorial Scholarship Fund

Directors

Richard K. LeBlond II, president

Thomas W. Burke, secretary and treasurer

Sir Michael Bonallack

William C. Campbell

Jack Nicklaus

Arnold Palmer

F. Morgan Taylor Jr.

Charles R. Yates

Committee

Andrew C. Bailey

Judy Bell

Stuart F. Bloch

Bradford R. Boss

W. Bradford Briggs

Thomas W. Chisholm

Theodore N. Danforth

E. Mandell de Windt

Melville P. Dickenson Jr.

Harry W. Easterly Jr.

Richard J. Fates

John W. Fischer III

Everett Risher

Gary A. Galyean

Robert M. Gardiner

C. Meade Geisel Jr.

H. James Griggs

Louis T. Hagoplan

Elbert O. Hand

William B. Harrison Jr.

Eugene M. Howerdd Jr.

Robert T. Jones IV

James R. Knerr

John D. Lauphaimor

David H. LeBlond

Martha V. Leonard

John T. Lupton

Sidney L. Matthew

Reg Murphy

Will F. Nicholson Jr.

Jaime Ortiz-Patino

Dr. John D. Reynolds

Daniel H. Ridder

Walter V. Shipley

John Staver

Jackson T. Stephens

Charles P. Stevenson

Hall W. Thompson

Robert N. Thompson

Ronald Townsend

Rayburn Tucker

Robert R. Waller, M.D.

Rawleigh Warner Jr.

Don M. Wilson III

Herbert Warren Wind

Bibliography

Alliance Theatre Company. *A Tribute to Bobby Jones*. Unpublished pamphlet, 1976.

"Amateur Golf Title: Mr. Bobby Jones Crowns His Record." *The Scotsman*, June 2, 1930.

"The American Championship." *The American Golfer*, October 1916.

"American Eagles and Birdies." *Outlook*, August 30, 1954, 12.

Anderson, Dave. "Golf's Bobby Jones Revival." *The New York Times*, April 14, 1996.

_____. "Methuselah of Masters Rates Personal Bests." *The New York Times*, April 12, 1998.

"Anglo-American Golf Final." *The Scotsman*, May 31, 1930.

"Another Jones Triumph." *The Scotsman*, July 15, 1927.

Armour, Tommy. "Pinshots of the Masters." *The American Golfer*, October 1935.

"Army Air Corps Captaincy Given to Bobby Jones." *Atlanta Journal*, June 9, 1942.

Aultman, Dick. "An Uncomplicated Approach." *Golf Digest*, April 1989, 164.

Bartlett, James Y. "The Golf Bag." *Forbes*, March 11, 1996, 69.

Behrand, John. *The Amateur: The Story of the Amateur Golf Championship, 1885–1995*. Worcestershire, Britain: Severnside Printers Ltd., 1995.

Bisher, Furman. "Bobby Jones Revisited." *Atlanta Magazine*, August 1963, 47.

_____. "The Gentleman Athlete." *Atlanta Journal*, December 20, 1971.

_____. "Golf's Teenage Sensation." *Golf Digest*, April 1965, 30.

_____. "The Southern Gentleman." *Golf* magazine, September 1960, 58.

Blodgett, Robert. "The King Tees Up for the Movies." *Golfers Magazine*, December 1930.

"Bob Jones in Britain but Not to Play Golf." *Atlanta Journal*, January 9, 1944.

"Bob Jones: Many Things to Many People." *Atlanta Journal-Constitution*, December 19, 1971.

"Bob Jones Ready for Minikhada." *Minneapolis Tribune*, August 21, 1927.

"Bobby Applies for Army Discharge." *Atlanta Constitution*, August 25, 1944.

"Bobby Beats Homans for Title as 10,000 Cheer." *Atlanta Journal*, September 28, 1930.

"Bobby 'Coasted In' Grantland Rice Says." *Atlanta Constitution*, September 25, 1930.

"Bobby Himself." *Atlanta Journal*, July 14, 1930.

"Bobby Jones Achieves His Ambition." *St. Andrews Citizen*, June 7, 1930.

"Bobby Jones, Amateur." *Outlook*, July 7, 1926, 336.

"Bobby Jones: America's Unofficial Ambassador." *The City Builder*, July 1930, 5.

"Bobby Jones and England." *The Living Age,* August 7, 1926, 335.

"Bobby Jones and the Duke of Windsor at Augusta, Georgia." *Atlanta Journal-Constitution*, May 18, 1952.

"Bobby Jones at Younger Hall: Complete Report of His Speech—Momentous and Historic Occasion." *St. Andrews Citizen*, October 18, 1958.

"Bobby Jones Begins Service in Air Corps." *Atlanta Journal*, June 24, 1942.

"Bobby Jones 'Champion Peter Pan': His Book." *The Literary Digest*, September 3, 1927, 38.

"Bobby Jones Confides How He Does It." *The Literary Digest*, July 31, 1926, 42.

"Bobby Jones Conquers the Golf World." *The Literary Digest*, July 30, 1927, 52.

"Bobby Jones' Gesture." *St. Andrews Citizen*, October 25, 1958.

"Bobby Jones' Grand Slam of Golf I: The British Amateur Championship." *Golf*, August 1965, 24.

"Bobby Jones' Grand Slam of Golf II: The British Open Championship." *Golf*, August 1965, 27.

"Bobby Jones' Grand Slam of Golf III: The United States Open Championship." *Golf*, August 1965, 29.

"Bobby Jones' Grand Slam of Golf IV: The United States Amateur Championship." *Golf*, August 1965, 32.

"Bobby Jones in Attendance at Ga-Fla Trials." *Thomasville Times-Enterprise*, February 17, 1938.

"Bobby Jones Is Here." *Dundee Courier & Advertiser*, April 25, 1936.

"Bobby Jones' Jeanie Deans." *Golf Digest*, September 1984.

"Bobby Jones Loses at Golf but Wins Affection of Others." *The Literary Digest*, April 7, 1934, 42.

"Bobby Jones Off for California." *Hearst* newspaper, August 18, 1929.

"Bobby Jones on His Victory." *Dundee Courier & Advertiser*, June 2, 1930.

"Bobby Jones on His Victory." *St. Andrews Citizen*, June 2, 1930.

"Bobby Jones: Only Golfer to Win Grand Slam Dies at 69." *The New York Times*, December 19, 1971.

"Bobby Jones Quits Law School and Will Enter Business Here Following Trip to New York." *Atlanta Constitution*, January 3, 1928.

"Bobby Jones Ready for Charity Match." *Los Angeles Herald Express*, March 24, 1931.

"Bobby Jones Still Idol of St. Andrews." *St. Andrews Citizen*, October 11, 1958.

"Bobby Jones Sues U.S. for Refund in Taxes on Income." *Los Angeles Times*, December 6, 1934.

"Bobby Jones: The Greatest Golfer." *The City Builder*, August 1927, 3.

"Bobby Jones: This Will Come First in My Heart." *Dundee Courier & Advertiser*, October 10, 1958.

"Bobby Jones Upsets Hollywood." *The Literary Digest*, April 18, 1931, 44.

"Bobby Jones Will Get Quarter Million for Moving Picture Work." *Atlanta Constitution*, November 18, 1930.

"Bobby Jones Wins British Amateur Golf Crown." *Atlanta Journal*, May 31, 1930, 1.

"Bobby Jones Wins Final Golf Crown of Year." *Montana Standard*, September 28, 1930.

"Bobby Jones Wins Fourth Title of Year, Reaching Ultimate Peak of Golf Glory." *Atlanta Constitution*, September 28, 1930.

"Bobby Jones Won Fame on the Golf Course but He Showed His True Greatness as a Man." *Atlanta Constitution*, March 17, 1954.

"Bobby Sees Old Course Again." *Dundee Courier & Advertiser*, October 4, 1958.

"Bobby Watching Waistline for Debut in the Movies." *Rochester New York Times-Union*, February 23, 1931.

Bowden, Ken. "Bobby Jones on Golf." *Golf Digest*, April 1990, 170.

Brennan, John M. "Bobby Jones and His Calamity Jane." *Metropolitan Golfer*, March 1952.

"The British Amateur." *USGA Golf Journal*, March 1971.

Browning, Robert. *A History of Golf: The Royal and Ancient Game.* London: J. M. Dent, 1955.

Burnes, Robert L. *50 Golden Years of Sports.* St. Louis: Rawlings Manufacturing Company, 1948.

Burnet, Bobby. *The St. Andrews' Opens.* Edinburgh: Sportsprints Publishers, 1990.

"Bygone Days." *The Commercial Appeal*, August 14, 1998.

Callaway, Ely. "Searching for Bobby Jones." *Time/Links*, March 1998.

Cantwell, Robert. "The Reel Life of Bobby Jones." *Sports Illustrated*, September 23, 1968.

"A Champion Returns to St. Andrews." *Sports Illustrated*, October 20, 1958, 34.

Clayton, Ward. "Callaway to Help Unveil Bobby Jones Sculpture Tonight." *Augusta Chronicle*, January 10, 1998.

_____. "The Pre-Masters." *Golf* magazine, April 1993, 108.

Cooke, Alistair. "What Have We Left for Bobby Jones?" *Golf Digest*, April 1996, 121.

"Cordial Welcome for Bobby Jones." *St. Andrews Citizen*, August 1, 1936.

Cotton, Henry. *A History of Golf Illustrated.* Philadelphia: Lippincott, 1975.

Cousins, Geoffrey. "Bobby Jones: Infant Prodigy to Golf Colossus." *London Daily Telegraph*, December 19, 1971.

Crawley, Leonard. "Bobby Jones the Master." *The Field*, October 16, 1958, 689.

Dale, Donoval. "Bob's Powder Not Damp, Danforth Says." *Atlanta Constitution*, July 11, 1930.

Dalyrimple, Dolly. "Dolly Interviews Bobby Jones' Boswell." *Birmingham News-Age Herald*, October 16, 1927.

Danzig, Allison and Peter Brandwein. *Sport's Golden Age.* New York: Harper and Brothers, 1948.

Darsie, Darsie L. "Green Tee." *Los Angeles Herald Express*, April 15, 1931.

Darwin, Bernard. "Bobby Jones Worship in England." *Vanity Fair*, July 1930, 70.

_____. *Golf Between Two Wars.* London: Chatto & Windus, 1944.

_____. *Green Memories.* London: Hodder & Stoughton, 1928.

_____. *The Complete Golfer: The Immortal Bobby.* New York: Simon & Schuster, 1954.

Davies, David. "Four Strokes That Shaped Lytham Lore." *Guardian*, July 17, 1996, 23.

_____. "The Jones Story Remains a Fascinating Open Book." *Guardian*, December 18, 1990, 13.

Davis, Bob. "Photobiography." *The American Golfer*, June 1935.

Davis, Evangeline. *The Lure of Highlands.* Highlands: Private publication by Highlands Country Club, 1981.

Davis, Martin. *The Greatest of Them All: The Legend of Bobby Jones.* Greenwich, Connecticut: American Golfer, Inc., 1996.

"The Decade: 1928–1937." *Golf* magazine, January 1988, 46.

Dey, Joseph C. Jr. "It Was Always Jones Against the Field." *Golf*, August 1965, 14.

Dobereiner, Peter. "Congregation of Champions." *Golf Digest*, June 1995, 128.

_____. "The Future Was Then." *Golf Digest*, March 1990, 98.

"Dogwood, Peaches, and a Man Named Jones." *Golf* magazine, April 1965, 26.

Doust, Dudley. "Museum Piece: A Brief History of the World's Most Famous Putter and Its Resurrection." *USGA Golf Journal*, 1976.

"Down in Four." *Time*, September 22, 1930.

Dreyspool, Joan Flynn. "Tommy Armour Analyzes the Jones Swing." *Golf*, September 1960.

"A Duffer's Consolation." *The American Golfer*, February 1931.

Durant, John, ed. *Yesterday in Sports.* New York: A. S. Barnes and Company, 1956, 94–105.

Durant, John, and Otto Bettman. *Pictorial History of American Sports.* New York: A. S. Barnes and Company, 1952, 192–97.

East, J. Victor. "Bobby Jones and His Calamity Jane." *Golf Digest*, May 1962.

"Eben Byers." *USGA Golf Journal*, October 1992.

"Eighteen Walker Cup Players Set for Bob Jones Tourney." *The Highlander*, July 28, 1998, 1.

Elliott, Charles. "Bobby Jones Gave Me a Fishing Lesson." *Atlanta Journal*, July 11, 1954.

_____. "Bobby Jones Gave Me a Fishing Lesson." *Atlanta Journal*, September 30, 1930.

_____. "Bobby Jones Gave Me a Fishing Lesson." *Atlanta Journal*, November 17, 1930.

_____. "Bobby Jones Gave Me a Fishing Lesson." *Atlanta Journal*, January 15, 1931.

_____. *East Lake Country Club*. Atlanta: Cherokee Publishing Co., 1984.

_____. *Mr. Anonymous*. Atlanta: Cherokee Publishing Co., 1982.

_____. *An Outdoor Life: The Autobiography of Charlie Elliott*. Atlanta: Flat Rock Press, 1994.

Emory University. The Robert Tyre Jones Jr. Memorial Lecture on Legal Ethics. Unpublished pamphlets, 1974–1999.

"Epic Putt Replayed." *Life*, October 18, 1954, 49.

Evans, Charles "Chick" Jr., with a foreword by Bobby Jones. *Chick Evans Golf Book*. New York: Thos. E. Wilson & Co., 1921.

Falls, Joe. "Jones Spoke with His Sticks." *Detroit News and Free Press*, April 7, 1996.

Farrell, L. A. "Massed Thousands Cheer for Bobby." *Atlanta Constitution*, July 15, 1930.

Fimrite, Ron. "The Emperor Jones." *Sports Illustrated*, April 11, 1994, 104.

Flaherty, Tom. *The Masters*. New York: Holt, Rinehart & Winston, 1961.

_____. *The U.S. Open 1895–1965*. New York: E. P. Dutton & Co., 1966.

"For Masters Only." *Time*, April 15, 1946, 62.

Fountain, Charles. *Sportswriter: The Life and Times of Grantland Rice*. New York: Oxford University Press, 1993.

Fraley, Oscar. "Springtime and Bobby Jones." *Golf* magazine, April 1964, 21.

Fraser, Alexa Stirling. "The Most Unforgettable Character I've Met." *Reader's Digest*, April 1960, 55.

Frost, Mark. *The Grand Slam: Bobby Jones, America, and the Story of Golf*. New York: Hyperion, 2004.

Gallico, Paul. *Farewell to Sport*. New York: Alfred A. Knopf, 1938.

_____. "The Golden People of a Golden Decade." *Chicago Tribune*, April 5, 1964.

_____. "Jones of Jonesville, Georgia." *Liberty*, October 26, 1929.

Ganem, Roger. "The Tools of Victory." *Golf*, August 1965, 38.

Gibson, Nevin. *The Encyclopedia of Golf with the Official All-Time Records*. New York: A. S. Barnes, 1958.

"Golden Anniversary of the Grand Slam." *Golf World*, February 22, 1980.

"Golden Jubilee of Golfing Grand Slam." *Dundee Courier & Advertiser*, February 16, 1980.

Golf magazine (Bobby Jones issue), September 1960.

Golf magazine (Grand Slam commemorative issue), August 1965.

The Golfer Magazine (Bobby Jones issue), March 1953.

"Golfer of the Golden Era." *Newsweek*, December 27, 1971.

"Golfer of the Half Century." *Golf World*, January 3, 1951.

Golfing Magazine Illustrated (Bobby Jones issue), September 1926.

"Golf's Conquering Hero Home Today." *Atlanta Constitution*, October 29, 1930.

Golf World News Weekly. (Masters issue), April 4, 1972.

Goodwin, Stephen. "Heroes for the Ages." *Golf* magazine, December 1997, 48.

Gordin, Richard Davis. "Robert Tyre Jones Jr.: His Life and Contributions to Golf." PhD diss., Ohio State University, 1967.

Gould, Alan. "Jones, 287, Wins Open, Mac Smith Second." *Los Angeles Examiner*, July 13, 1930.

Gould, Dave. "Spalding from the Beginning." *Golf Illustrated*, March 1991.

Graffis, Herb. (The Grand Slam Anniversary issue), *Golfing*, April 1960.

Green, Kell. *The Golf Swing of Bobby Jones: An Analysis of His Drive*. Chicago: Dixon Press, 1931.

Gregory, C. E. "O. B. Keeler Is Given Watch and Honorary Membership by the Associated Press." *Atlanta Journal*, August 19, 1926.

Griffin, George C. "Bob Jones, Class of '22." *Georgia Tech Alumnus*, Winter 1972.

Grizzard, Lewis. "Letter from Jones Landed the Open." *Atlanta Journal*, October 8, 1972.

Gwin, Yolande. "Bobby Jones Room." *Atlanta Journal-Constitution*, June 13, 1976.

Hanley, Reid. "A Master: Bobby Jones Golf Video." *Chicago Tribune*, March 10, 1989.

Hannigan, Frank. "The Lost Letters of Bobby Jones." *Golf Digest*, April 1994, 108.

_____. "The Power Broker: From Inventing the Masters to Electing a President, Clifford Roberts Knew How to Pull All the Right Levers." *Golf Digest*, April 1996, 146.

Harris, Robert. *Sixty Years of Golf*. London: Batchworth Press, 1953.

Harrison, Dave. "Jones Didn't Feel Ready for U.S. Open, But. . . ." *Augusta Chronicle-Herald*, April 2, 1972.

"Hoover Greets Bobby Wishes Him Success in American Amateur." *Atlanta Constitution*, September 16, 1930.

"How Bobby Jones Overcame His Temper." *Liberty*, June 7, 1924, 3.

"How Many More Titles Are in Store for 'Our Bobby'?" *The Literary Digest*, September 17, 1927, 63.

Howard, Jock. "The Man Who Knows More About Bobby Jones Than Any One Else in the World." *Golf World*, April 1998.

"Is Bobby Jones Losing Interest in Golf?" *The Literary Digest*, September 21, 1929, 66.

Jackson, Teague. "Flood of Eulogies Pours in for Jones." *Atlanta Constitution*, December 19, 1971.

_____. "Masters Just Not Quite the Same Without Jones." *Atlanta Journal-Constitution*, April 9, 1972.

_____. "This Summer's U.S. Open Dedicated to Bobby Jones." *Atlanta Journal-Constitution*, March 16, 1969.

Jenkins, Dan. "The Masters: Bobby Jones Started It All." *Sports Illustrated*, April 6, 1978.

_____. "My Lists of Golf's Greatest Moments." *Golf Digest*, July 1996, 40.

"Jones and Ravielli." *Golf Digest*, August 1969.

Jones, Ben Perry. *Robert Tyre Jones: A Family Perspective*. Canton, Georgia: privately printed, 1990.

"The Jones Complex on the Golf Links." *The Literary Digest*, October 6, 1928.

"Jones Explains How to Play Whitfield Course." *Sarasota Herald-Tribune*, December 19, 1925.

"Jones Graveside Services at Oakland Are Private." *Atlanta Journal*, December 20, 1971.

"Jones Is Mourned at Scottish Links." *The New York Times*, December 19, 1971.

"Jones Nears L.A. Enroute for Amateur." *Hearst* newspaper, August 20, 1929.

Jones, Paul. "Swinging with Bobby Jones." *Atlanta Constitution*, May 1, 1975.

"Jones Returns to Atlanta on Par with Ben Franklin." *Atlanta Constitution*, October 15, 1958.

Jones, Robert Trent. "Atlanta's New Peachtree Is Pretested by Bobby Jones." *Golfdom*, March 1949, 61.

Jones, Robert Tyre Jr. *Bobby Jones on Golf.* Garden City, New York: Doubleday and Co., 1966.

_____. *Bobby Jones on the Basic Golf Swing.* New York: Doubleday, 1969.

_____. *Golf Is My Game.* Garden City, New York: Doubleday and Co., 1960.

_____. "Goodbye to Golf." *Liberty*, January 31, 1931.

_____. *How to Run a Golf Tournament.* New York: American Golf Institute, ca. 1936.

_____. "Joy for the Average, Test for the Expert." *Sports Illustrated*, April 6, 1959, 38.

_____. "Learn How to Stroke the Ball." *The American Golfer*, June 1931.

_____. "Not My Business." *Colliers*, April 26, 1930.

_____. *Rights and Wrongs of Golf.* New York: A. G. Spalding and Co., 1935.

_____. "St. Andrews Course Most Fascinating of All." *Atlanta Constitution*, June 8, 1927.

Jones, Robert Tyre Jr. and O. B. Keeler. *Down the Fairway.* New York: Minton Balch & Co., 1927.

_____. *How I Play Golf.* New York: American Sport Publishing Co., 1935.

Jones, Robert Tyre Jr., W. D. Richardson, and Lincoln Werden. "The Ideal Golf Course." *Annual Golf Review Illustrated*, 1932.

"Jones Triumphs Again." *Outlook*, September 7, 1927, 6.

"Jones Wins Amateur Crown for Grand Slam." *Dallas Morning News*, September 28, 1930.

"Jones Wins British Open Third Time." *Chicago Daily News*, June 20, 1930.

Keeler, O. B. *The Autobiography of an Average Golfer.* New York: Greenberg Publishing, 1925.

_____. "Bob Jones Off to U.S. Amateur." *Atlanta Constitution*, September 16, 1930.

_____. "Bobby Jones Deserts Calamity Jane for 'Mike'." *Atlanta Journal*, January 11, 1931.

_____. "Bobby Jones' Golf Swing." *Atlanta Journal-Constitution*, June 29, 1947.

_____. "Bobby Jones Wins National Open." *Outdoor South*, August 1923.

_____. *The Boy's Life of Bobby Jones.* New York: Harper & Brothers, 1931.

_____. "Gallery Gasps as Gunn Sinks 120-Foot Putt." *Atlanta Journal*, June 3, 1926.

_____. "The Grand Slam." *Golf*, September 1960, 31.

_____. "Golf Gossip." *Outdoor South*, March 1926.

_____. "Golf Gossip: The Director Gets an Idea for the Bobby Jones Movies." *American Golfer*, March 1931.

_____. "Jones and Adam Win Match." *Outdoor South*, September 1923.

_____. "Jones Writes More History." *The American Golfer*, August 1930.

_____. "Jones Tied Record to Lead Amateur Field." *Atlanta Constitution*, September 24, 1930.

_____. "Looking at the South." *Golf Review Illustrated*, 1923, 37.

_____. "O. B. Finds Historic Spot Where Wallace Crawled to Die at Stirling Castle." *Atlanta Journal*, May 30, 1926.

_____. "Old England's Ideal Spot." *Atlanta Constitution*, May 18, 1976.

_____. "More Than 100 Aces Made at East Lake: Jones Got Two." *Atlanta Constitution*, September 20, 1949.

_____. "The National Amateur Championship." *Outdoor South*, October 1925, 3.

_____. "St. Andrews Course Most Fascinating of All." *Dundee Courier & Advertiser*, October 10, 1958.

_____. "Shoot the Works Says Stewart Maiden." *The American Golfer*, December 27, 1924.

_____. "Today's Jones." *Golfing*, March 1941.

Keeler, O. B., and Grantland Rice. *The Bobby Jones Story.* Atlanta: Tupper & Love, 1953.

Kenny, H. F. "Secrets of the Master: The Best of Bobby Jones." *Choice*, July 1997.

Kertes, Stan, and Betty Hicks. "Hogan vs. Jones." *Golf Digest*, April 1955, 32.

Kindred, Dave. "Birthplace of a Legend." *Golf* magazine, April 1994, 24.

_____. "Bobby Jones Made It So." *Sporting News*, April 13, 1998.

King, Augusta Wylie. "Golf as First Played in Atlanta." *Atlanta Historical Bulletin*, December 8, 1947, 9–11.

Kinney, Bill. "Keeler and Bobby Jones." *Marietta Daily Journal*, August 28, 1975.

_____. "Keeler, the Storyteller, in Demand." *Marietta Daily Journal*, August 29, 1975.

Kirker, Thomas. "Pen Pals." *Golf* magazine, April 1989, 80.

Krout, John Allen. *Annals of American Sport.* New Haven: Yale University Press, 1929, 280–96.

Kupelian, Vartan. "Film Reflects Jones' Spirit." *Detroit News and Free Press*, April 7, 1996.

_____. "Jones Biography Tops 95 Leaderboard." *Detroit News*, November 21, 1995.

Laney, Al. "He Does Not Live in the Past but in the Present of Golf." *Golf Digest*, March 1972.

Lewis, Catherine M. *Considerable Passions: Golf, the Masters, and the Legacy of Bobby Jones.* Chicago: Triumph Books, 2000.

Lieber, Jill. "Legend, Mentor, Friend: Celebrated Man Behind Masters Is Lovingly Remembered." *USA Today*, April 8, 1997.

"Like Father, Like Fun." *Time*, May 12, 1941, 56.

Lonetree, Anthony. "Studies in Character." *Minneapolis Star Tribune*, April 9, 1996.

Longhurst, Henry. "Bobby in Britain." *Golf*, September 1960, 17.

_____. "He Belongs to Us, Too." *Golf*, August 1965, 18.

_____. "A Sad Loss." *London Sunday Times*, December 19, 1971.

"Loss to St. Andrews: Passing of Bobby Jones." *St. Andrews Citizen*, December 20, 1971.

Lowe, Steven. *Sir Walter and Mr. Jones: Walter Hagen, Bobby Jones, and the Rise of American Golf*. Ann Arbor, Michigan: Sleeping Bear Press, 2000.

Lowenberer, William. "Local Golf Veteran Remembers Bob Jones." *Baltimore Sun*, December 19, 1971.

Ludwick, Al. "Jones Started 1930 Streak in Augusta." *Augusta Chronicle-Herald*, April 2, 1972.

MacKenzie, Alister. *The Spirit of St. Andrews*. Chelsea, Michigan: Sleeping Bear Press, 1995.

Maiden, Stewart. "A Lesson in Golf." *Outdoor South*, December 1923.

_____. "A Lesson in Golf: The Chip Shot." *Outdoor South*, September 1923, 10.

_____. "A Lesson in Golf: Putting." *Outdoor South*, August 1923, 15.

_____. "A Lesson in Golf: The Medium Pitch." *Outdoor South*, October 1923, 18.

_____. "Tips for the Round." *Outdoor South*, May 1925.

Martin, H. B. *Fifty Years of American Golf*. New York: Dodd, Mead, 1936.

"The Masters." *Sports Illustrated*, April 6, 1959.

Matthew, Sidney L. "Along Came Jones." *The 1995 Masters Journal*, April 6–9, 1995, 120.

_____. "The Birth of Bobby's Dream Course." *Links*, April 1999, 54.

_____. "Bobby Jones' Calamity Janes I and II." *Golfiana* 4 (1992): 3–11.

_____. *Bobby Jones Golf Tips*. Chelsea, Michigan: Sleeping Bear Press, 1999.

_____. "Bobby Jones' March on St. Andrews." *St. Andrews and Golf*. Cincinnati: Market Street Press, 1995.

_____. *Champions of East Lake: Bobby Jones and Friends*. Tallahassee, Florida: I.Q. Press, 1999.

_____. "Dreams Die Hard." *British Golf Monthly*, IPC Magazine, April 1998, 95.

_____. "Essay on the Symmetrical and Balanced Theme." N.p.: privately printed, 1994.

_____. "First Pictorial History of Bobby Jones Original Hickories 1926–1930." *Golf Collectors' Society Bulletin,* November 1985.

_____. "Golf's Unsung Genius: Frank Sampson." Centel Classic. N.p.: Centel Corporation, 1989.

_____. "Impeccable Bobby Jones." *The Country Club*. Canaan, Connecticut: Club Publications, Inc., 1996.

_____. "The Legacy of American Golf." *Fine Art of America's Fairways*. N.p.: Fine Art of the Fairway, Ltd., 1998.

_____. *The Life and Times of Bobby Jones*. Chelsea, Michigan: Sleeping Bear Press, 1995.

_____. "The Life and Times of Bobby Jones." *Golf* magazine, April 1996, 92.

_____. "Luck or Destiny?" *1997 Andersen Consulting World Championship of Golf*. Largo, Florida: ISM Group, Inc., 1997.

_____. *Secrets of the Master: The Best of Bobby Jones*. Chelsea, Michigan: Sleeping Bear Press, 1996.

_____. "Timeless Tips from a Legend." *The 1997 Masters Journal*, April 7–13, 1997, 118.

_____. "Who Stole Bobby Jones' Clubs?" *1996 Andersen Consulting World Championship of Golf*. Largo, Florida: ISM Group, Inc., 1996.

McAndrew, Harry. "Why Bobby Jones Aimed to Hit the Crowd." *Glasgow Scottish Sunday Express*, June 9, 1957.

McCollister, Tom. "60 Years Ago Bobby Jones Made History." *Atlanta Constitution*, September 27, 1990.

McGill, Ralph. "Bobby Jones: Great Man and Great Golfer." *Atlanta Journal-Constitution*, March 15, 1953.

"In Memory of Bobby Jones." *St. Andrews Citizen*, August 8, 1972.

"I Met a Man . . ." *Dundee Courier & Advertiser*, October 13, 1958.

Middleton, Drew. "'Welcome Home Bobby,' Scots Cry." *Atlanta Constitution*, October 4, 1958.

Miles, Ed. "Bonnie Bobby: Golfer of the Ages." *Southern Living*, April 1972.

_____. "Final Tribute Accorded Keeler by Sports World." *Atlanta Journal*, October 16, 1950.

_____. "Jones Completes Masterpiece." *Atlanta Journal-Constitution*, September 18, 1960.

_____. "Thirty Five Years Later." *Golf Digest*, August 1965, 50.

Miller, Richard. *Triumphant Journey: The Saga of Bobby Jones and the Grand Slam of Golf*. New York: Holt, Rinehart & Winston, 1980.

Moon, Fred. "Big Bob Talks of Little Bob." *Atlanta Journal*, August 3, 1930.

"Mr. Bobby Jones' Great Golf." *The Scotsman*, May 27, 1930.

"Muffled Grief Pays Tribute to Way Bob Jones Lived." *Atlanta Journal*, December 21, 1971.

Murray, Jim. "A Major Success." *Golf* magazine, April 1998, 24.

Neill, Nancy. *More Than Bricks and Mortar: A History of the Atlanta Athletic Club*. Atlanta: W. H. Wolfe, 1987.

"The New Burgess of St. Andrews." *St. Andrews Citizen*, October 11, 1958.

"The New Golf Champion." *Outlook*, September 29, 1926, 137.

Newberry, Kevin. "Jones: Golf's Best Eternally an Amateur." *Houston Post*, August 22, 1993.

Nicklaus, Jack with Herbert Warren Wind. *The Greatest Game of All: My Life in Golf*. New York: Simon & Schuster, 1969.

Nicklaus, Jack with Ken Bowden. "Bob Jones Remembered." *Golf* magazine, April 1995, 73.

_____. "My Favorite Lessons from Bobby Jones." *Golf Digest*, May 1989, 120.

"And Now Bobby Jones Plans to Golf for Pleasure." *The Literary Digest*, October 11, 1930.

"O. B. Keeler Tells Story of Fishing for Tarpon Here." *Sarasota Herald*, August 1, 1926.

"Obituary: Bobby Jones." *Atlanta Constitution*, December 19, 1971.

"The Old Course at St. Andrews." *Strokesaver*. London: Ducam Mtg. UK Ltd., 1990.

"Open Championship." *The Scotsman*, July 12, 1927.

"Open Championship." *The Scotsman*, July 13, 1927.

"Open Golf Championship A Day of Thrills." *The Scotsman*, June 24, 1921.

"Open Golf Championship Bobby Jones' Great Triumph." *St. Andrews Citizen*, July 23, 1927.

"Open Golf Title: Mr. Jones Still Leads." *The Scotsman*, July 13, 1927.

Ouimet, Francis. *A Game of Golf: A Book of Reminiscences*. Boston: Houghton Mifflin, 1932.

Outlar, Jesse. "Amateur Made Atlanta Major Sports City." *Atlanta Constitution*, September 28, 1930.

_____. "A Simple Service." *Atlanta Constitution*, December 21, 1971.

"Packed Hall Sees Freedom Ceremony at St. Andrews." *Dundee Courier & Advertiser*, October 10, 1958.

"Par Wasn't Good Enough When Farrell Beat Bobby for the Open." *The Literary Digest*, July 7, 1928, 52.

Parham, Betty. "Dixie Memories: Golf." *Atlanta Journal*, March 10, 1985.

Park, Hugh. "Great Golfer Is Honored." *Atlanta Journal*, November 12, 1976.

Paxton, Harry and Fred Russell. "A Visit with Bobby Jones." *Saturday Evening Post*, April 1958.

Peper, George. *Golf in America: The First One Hundred Years*. New York: Harry N. Abrams, Inc., 1994.

_____. *Grand Slam Golf*. New York: Harry N. Abrams, 1991.

_____. "Keeping Up with Jones." *Golf* magazine, August 1989, 8.

"The Perfect Amateur." *Outlook*, July 21, 1926, 399.

Perkerson, Medora. "How Bobby Will Make Movies." *Atlanta Journal*, February 8, 1931.

Perry, Ben. *Robert Tyre Jones: A Family Perspective*. Canton, Georgia: Privately printed, 1990.

"Player of the Decade: Robert Tyre Jones Jr." *Golf* magazine, January 1988, 48.

Pottinger, George. *Muirfield and the Honourable Company*. Edinburgh: Scottish Academic Press, 1972.

Powers, Francis J. "Bobby Jones Retires from Competitive Golf." *Golfers Magazine*, December 1930.

Pratt, J. Lowell, ed. *Sport, Sport, Sport*. New York: J. Lowell Pratt Company, 1963.

Price, Charles. *The American Golfer*. New York: Random House, 1964.

_____. "Bobby Jones Reveals His Inner Psychology." *Golf Digest*, August 1989, 40.

_____. "The Champ." *Review*, March 1980, 24.

_____. "From Merion to Merion." *Golf*, September 1960, 14.

_____. *A Golf Story: Bobby Jones, Augusta National, and the Masters Tournament*. New York: Atheneum, 1986.

_____. "The Last Days of Bobby Jones." *Golf Digest*, April 1991, 184.

_____. "Robert Tyre 'Bobby' Jones: The Head Master 1902–1971." *Golf*, April 1972, 49.

_____. "Sir Walter and the Emperor Jones." *Golf Digest*, April 1992, 58.

_____. *The World of Golf*. New York: Random House, 1962.

Price, Charles, et. al. "The Bobby Jones Issue." *Golf*, September 1960.

Rabinowitz, Howard. "Bob Jones' First Retirement." *USGA Golf Journal*, May 1993.

Rader, Benjamin G. *American Sports: From the Age of Folk Games to the Age of Televised Sports*. Upper Saddle River, New Jersey: Prentice Hall, 1999.

Range, Willard. "P. J. Berckmans: Georgia Horticulturist." *Georgia Review* (Summer 1952): 219.

Rice, Grantland. "Bobby Jones on Golf." New York: Bell Syndicate, 1930.

_____. *The Bobby Jones Story: From the Writings of O. B. Keeler*. Atlanta: Tupper and Love, 1953.

_____. "Interviewing Horton Smith." *The American Golfer*, June 1930.

_____. "Jones an Artist." *The New York Times*, June 19, 1926.

_____. "Scots Hailed Jones' Return." *Atlanta Journal-Constitution*, December 19, 1971.

_____. "Untrod Ground." *The American Golfer*, November 1930.

Richardson, William D. and Lincoln A. Werden. *The Golfer's Year Book*. New York: The Golfer's Year Book, 1931.

"Robert Tyre Jones (1902–1971): 'We Always Play the Ball as It Lies.'" *The Decorator's Show House*. Atlanta: Atlanta Symphony Orchestra, 1991, 18.

Roberts, Charles. "Bobby Jones: Man, Legend." *Atlanta Journal-Constitution*, December 19, 1971.

_____. "Jones Ignored Weather in '33, Shot 67, Tops Until Bulla's 65." *Atlanta Journal-Constitution*, February 8, 1948.

Roberts, Clifford. *The Story of the Augusta National Golf Club*. New York: Doubleday and Co., 1976.

"R. T. Jones Double: Stirring Finish at Hoylake." *London Times*, June 21, 1930.

Ruark, Robert C. "Atlanta's Bobby Jones Has Earned Immortality as a Great Sportsman." *Atlanta Constitution*, September 21, 1949.

Russell, Fred. "Bobby Jones' Favorite Masters Experience." *Tennessean*, April 9, 1998.

Ryde, Peter. *Strokesaver: The Official Course Guide for the Old Course at St. Andrews*. Glasgow, Scotland: Stroke Sports Leisure Products/The Royal St. George's Golf Club, 1981.

"A Sad Loss." *London Sunday Times*, December 19, 1971.

"St. Andrews Greets Champ Bobby Jones." *Atlanta Constitution*, October 4, 1958.

Salinger, H. G. "Jones Changes Mind About St. Andrews." *London Sunday Times*, May 17, 1930.

Salmond, J. B. *The Story of the R&A Being the History of the First Two Hundred Years of the Royal and Ancient Golf Club of St. Andrews*. London: MacMillan, 1956.

Saporta, Maria. "Local Executives Honor Memory of Golf Legend." *Atlanta Journal-Constitution*, June 2, 1998.

Sarazen, Gene with Herbert Warren Wind. *Thirty Years of Championship Golf: The Life and Times of Gene Sarazen*. New York: Prentice-Hall, 1950.

Schrock, Cliff. "Bobby Jones' Last Major." *Golf Digest*, April 1990, 113.

_____. "A Fellow Star Remembers Bobby Jones." *Golf Digest*, May 1991, 52.

Seelig, Pat. "Jones vs. Hagen." *Golf* magazine, January 1993, 62.

Sheridan, James. *Sheridan of Sunningdale: My Fifty-Six Years as a Caddie Master.* London: Country Life, 1967.

Shiffman, Roger. "Classic Instruction." *Golf Digest*, June 1998, 52.

"Shots Out of Hell and Other Satanic Bunkers." *Golf World*, May 1994.

Sibley, John. "The Strength of Ethics." Reprint of the Robert Tyre Jones Jr. Memorial Lecture on Legal Ethics, Emory University Law School, Atlanta, Georgia, March 29, 1979.

Smith, Horton and Dawson Taylor, with a foreword by Bobby Jones. *The Secret of Holing Putts*. New York: A. S. Barnes & Co., 1961.

Smith, Red. "Fore!" *American Heritage*, August 1980.

Sommers, Robert. "Bobby Jones: The Grand Slam." *Golf* magazine, May 1995, 131.

_____. *Golf Anecdotes*. New York: Oxford Press, 1995.

"The Southern Gentleman." *Golf*, August 1965, 35.

Spiker, Lawrence J. III. "A National Championship Comes to SAE." *The Record of Sigma Alpha Epsilon*, October 1923, 103.

Steel, Donald. "The Master." *Sunday Telegraph*, December 19, 1971.

Stiles, Maxwell. "Bobby Ready for Start of Film Career." *Los Angeles Times*, March 2, 1931.

_____. "Jones Arrives, Plays Lakeside." *Hearst* newspapers, August 22, 1929.

Stump, Al. "History: Bobby and Ty." *Golf* magazine, April 1990, 68.

Symms, R. D. "Bobby Jones: Portrait of a Gentleman." *The Record of Sigma Alpha Epsilon*, Summer 1996, 4.

Tarde, Jerry. "Bobby Jones's Reputation Still Growing." *The New York Times*, April 9, 1990.

Taylor, Dawson. *The Masters: Golf's Most Prestigious Tradition*. New Jersey: A. S. Barnes, 1981.

_____. *St. Andrews: Cradle of Golf*. New Jersey: A. S. Barnes, 1976.

"Testing Different Putting Stances." *The American Golfer*, June 1931.

"Thief Steals Bobby Jones' Prized Clubs." *Los Angeles Times*, May 30, 1929.

Thompson, Jimmy. "Yesterday's Golfers Were Better." *Golf*, April 1965, 18.

Thomy, Al. "Jones Returns to City Holding Fifth 'Freedom.'" *Atlanta Constitution*, October 15, 1958.

Tolhurst, Desmond. "A Most Beautiful Friendship." *Golf*, December 1993, 84.

Tolley, Cyril J. H. *The Modern Golfer*. New York: Alfred A. Knopf, 1924.

"Tommy Armour Analyzes the Jones Swing." *Golf*, August 1965, 25.

Townsend, James L. "Bobby Jones Is Dead." *Georgia*, January 1971, 11.

"Tracking the 100 Greatest." *Golf Digest*, May 1995, 106.

Trevor, George. "A Little Flyer on Bobby." *Outlook and Independent*, September 24, 1930, 227.

"Triumph for Amateur Golf." *Dundee Courier & Advertiser*, June 25, 1921.

Turbeville, R. T., ed. Eminent Georgians. *Atlanta: Southern Society for Research and History*, 1937.

"25 Greats Pick Their Top Ten." *Golf Digest*, January 1996, 80.

"Unique Old Course Ceremony." *St. Andrews Citizen*, September 16, 1972.

Ward-Thomas, Pat. *The Royal and Ancient*. Edinburgh: Scottish Academic Press, 1980.

Wethered, Roger H. "My Impressions of Bobby Jones." *The American Golfer*, January 1931.

Index